"WISHING You JOY, WEALTH, + Success"

Frank & Marilynn

HEROISMS™

8 PILLARS TO A LIFE OF
PASSION, BEAUTY & CREATIVITY

PETER BORONKAY

Library and Archives Canada Cataloguing in Publication is available upon request.

Paperback ISBN: 978-1-777-3466-0-7

ebook ISBN: 978-1-777-3466-1-4

Photo credits courtesy of:

Canadian Olympic Committee - Olympic Academy of Canada

Dave Roels - Photographer - Bill Clinton

Loyola High School

Matt Nest - Photographer - Peter Boronkay

Peter Nilas - Photographer - Wedding

TEDx Abbotsford

Toronto Stock Exchange

Published by Amazon Kindle Direct Publishing

To Geraldine, for her love and patience while we explore a life of HEROISMS.

TABLE OF CONTENTS

INTRODUCTION - HEROISMS 1

CHAPTER ONE - Background 5

CHAPTER TWO - 100 Life Visions 27

    Seasonality of Life..30

8 PILLARS OF HEROISMS 31

CHAPTER THREE - HEALTH – The First Wealth 33

    Medical...33

    Fitness...37

    Nutrition 38

CHAPTER FOUR - EDUCATION – Life-Long Learning........ 39

    College..39

    Undergraduate..40

    Graduate 41

    Professional 42

CHAPTER FIVE - RELATIONS – Family and Friends............ 45

    Bachelor 45

    Family...51

        Marriage – A Unity of Souls 51

Parenthood 54

Family Relations.. 63

Friends..74

CHAPTER SIX - OCCUPATION – Your Mission **79**

Starting Out..79

Lifeguard 79

White-Water Rafting Guide............................. 81

Career 82

Computers 82

Computers and Architecture........................... 84

Wealth Management 85

CHAPTER SEVEN - INTERESTS – The Spice of Life **97**

Sports..97

Hockey 97

Running 99

Martial Arts 101

Swimming... 103

Skiing.. 106

Curling 108

Golf... 111

Motorcycling 113

Creative Expression...115

Hypnosis 115

Music 116

Temple of Love.. 119

Reading and Writing 123

Cottage Life...124

Canoe Trip on Forest Lake Loop 133

Travel...135

Pope John Paul II at the Vienna Airport 138

Blizzard on the Icefield's Parkway.................. 139

Marooned on Jedediah Island 140

CHAPTER EIGHT - SOCIETY – Our Interconnectedness.... **143**

Olympics and Paralympics...143

    Montreal 1976...144

    Calgary 1988 145

    Olympic Academy of Canada 2004.....................146

    Torino 2006..147

    Beijing 2008...148

    Vancouver 2010..151

Meeting a US President 156

TEDx Abbotsford 158

Making a Difference..161

CHAPTER NINE - MONEY - A Means to Your Visions **163**

Financial Independence..165

Emotions and Investing...166

Investing Revisited 166

Asset Allocation...167

Six Investment Models™...167

    Fixed Income 168

    Equities 168

    Alternatives 174

    Sustainable Investing 175

How Younger Investors May Build a $1Million Portfolio.....175

Real Estate..176

    Home 176

    Cottage..178

    Investment 178

CHAPTER TEN - SPIRITUALITY – Your Inner Journey **181**

    Being in the moment 182

    Positive Attitude 182

    Meditation 183

    Openness to your true self 184

    Interconnectedness 184

    Learning 185

EPILOGUE **187**

ABOUT THE AUTHOR **189**

APPENDIX **191**

    A: 100 Life Visions 191

    B: Health History 195

    C: Countries Visited 196

    D: Tax-free Savings Account Scenarios 200

    E: Peace – Fourth Proposed Olympic Pillar 202

SOURCES **207**

HEROISMS

"Boldness has genius, power, and magic in it."

Goethe

Each year between Christmas and New Year's I reserve a day of solitude where I sit by a crackling wood fire, sip a finely aged glass of Tuscan Cabernet Sauvignon, watch snowflakes dance on our windowpanes, and reflect on my 100 Life Visions.

The purpose of this list is to stay on track with what I want to engineer in my life. I also establish ten goals to accomplish in the coming year. I take two goals from my 100 Life Visions and then set another eight goals to achieve during the calendar year. I choose ten goals because, with 12 months in the year, I allow myself two free months as a break from the continual effort.

At the time of this writing I have accomplished 82 of my 100 Life Visions. By tackling two life aspirations a year I may be able to complete my list within a decade.

Sir Isaac Newton and Shakespeare wrote their best works during plagues, and that inspired me to push ahead and complete this book during the COVID-19 global pandemic of 2020. The purpose of this book is to provide you with a framework for answering the following question: Should you focus on the grand vision for your life or your day-to-day tasks?

I have observed that many people display well-organized agendas prominently on their desks. Appointments, errands, and projects are clearly listed, but when the person is asked about their overall life plan, a clear answer is often lacking. I maintain that your life vision requires your dedicated attention to enable you to pursue an optimal existence on your own terms.

When I was 26 years old, the inspiration to live my visions led me to start a journal that I have kept up for over 32 years. My writings evolved from daily thoughts and observations to big picture thinking, which led me to develop a system for reflecting on my life goals, first putting them in writing and then executing them.

HEROISMS is an acronym for the eight pillars that support reflection and planning. These pillars are: Health, Education, Relations, Occupation, Interests, Society, Money, and Spirituality.

All aspects of your life may be incorporated into these pillars. Like many people, you may be over-confident about what you may achieve in the short term but underestimate what may be accomplished in a lifetime.

From white-water rafting to portfolio management I write to you my learning lessons on life with anecdotes, insights, and practical takeaways. I invite you to use this book to help you boldly tackle life on your own terms so that you can pursue your own HEROISMS.

CHAPTER ONE

BACKGROUND

My parents immigrated to Canada from Hungary in 1951 after a three-year stay in Switzerland. My father, Dénes, a lawyer by education, and my mother, Margit, a dress designer and artist, left their homeland in Budapest along with their children after the communist takeover in 1948 and sought out better opportunities. They settled in Ottawa and lived on a side street beside the Governor General's residence. My brother Denis told me how he used to play on the grounds of the Queen's representative and sometimes an RCMP officer would come by to check what he and his friends were up to. My mother was introduced to a strong network in Ottawa. Two wives of Canadian prime ministers, Mrs. Pearson and Mrs. Diefenbaker commissioned dresses from her. My mother once said that both women, who were from different political parties, came over to our house to meet on neutral ground and discuss political matters. After a good start in Ottawa my family moved to Montreal so my mother could be closer to her sister, who was the first member of the family to come to Canada.

My parents 1942

Moving from an established noble life in Hungary to WWII, then followed by the communist takeover was horrific enough for my parents but difficulties indeed tragedies did not end there while setting up a new life in Canada. My parents had a daughter, Julia, born in 1956; however she passed away in 1959 from a hole in the heart birth defect. My mother and father had first-hand experience in black swan events that derailed their lives. This did not stop them from fighting to move forward. This leads me to the main idea of this book: that even in the most difficult circumstances, you must strive to pursue a meaningful life of competence in each of your life pillars of HEROISMS.

I came into this world on April 29, 1962 and at the time my family at the time lived in an attractive stone-faced home that they rented at 29 Bruce Avenue in Westmount close to downtown Montreal. When I was only two years old my father took a reference law librarian post at Harvard University and we moved to 99 Newtonville Ave., Newton, a suburb of Boston. My first recollection in life was at age two when my father was driving and he pointed to the house where our family would live in this established hilly neighborhood I grew up in until age eight.

After four years in Massachusetts, my father, then 53 fulfilled his dream of buying a country property near Stowe, Vermont. I shared his deep passion for country living

Four years old, Newton, Mass., 1966

and later, Geraldine and I bought our own place on a lake on the Sunshine Coast, BC when I was 48. While in Boston, I attended a preschool in Chestnut Hill where deep piles of fall leaves were gathered for pick-up along a road of towering mature trees that stretched over, creating a canopy over the road. Jumping in and out of the leaves is delightful when you are five. One day when my father was collecting fall leaves into large bags on a grassy slope across the street from our home, I thought it a good idea to use the bags of leaves as target practice for a bow and arrow I had received as a gift. I took aim from the other side of the road to shoot, well away from my father but the arrow curved to the right and pierced one of the large bags very close to my father's left side. It was fortunate that he did not notice and I was able to retrieve the arrow without earning his legendary wrath.

In 1969 I watched the events surrounding the Apollo 11 landing on the moon. After the astronauts touched down, Neil Armstrong finally emerged from the capsule at 10:56 p.m. EST, though I had to go to bed before that iconic moment. I am sure that as a seven-year-old kid and hearing this news of the millennium, I was not alone in wanting to be an astronaut at that time. That same year the Boeing 747 airplane was close to being introduced into commercial service and a cereal brand had taken up a promotion to receive a model of that plane if you sent in three box flaps. As soon as the groceries arrived, I cut out the flaps to send away. I was thrilled to receive the model 747 plane in the mail soon after. Although I enjoyed living in Massachusetts, in 1970 my mother decided to move back to Montreal to be close to her sister and away from my father, as they were on the verge of separating, likely due to my father's difficult temperament, one that was impacted by his life's challenging circumstances.

I was eight years old when my mother and I moved back from Boston to Montreal. With my parents' separation there was a noticeable decline in the financial standard of living we had enjoyed previously. My father did move up to join us, but after two years my parents permanently separated, though they never divorced. After decades apart they would again live in the same building but in different rooms at St. Margaret's seniors' home in Westmount until my father passed away at 97 ½ in 2012 and my mother at 99 in 2017. Although they did not get to see 100, they came close. I researched the actuarial odds of a married couple both living to 100 and it was 1 in 6 million! Because of this many people comment that I have good genes, and I hope they are right. However, in high school I ate too much junk food that I hope I have since recovered from.

My two brothers and sister were mostly out of the house by now being 26, 25, and 22 years old, while I was only eight. Months later in October, the FLQ (Front de Libération du Québec) crisis was in full swing with kidnappings occurring and the War Measures Act in place. There were no shortages of political drama that my parents had to endure. I was old enough to understand that there were problems going on but none that affected me personally. I was happy to swim at the Montreal West pool, or during the winter, play hockey or toboggan at Murray Hill Park in Westmount. Years later, I worked during summers as a tennis court attendant and a lifeguard also for the City of Westmount.

My first of a few street fights took place when a classmate in grade four challenged me to a brawl after school in the winter. A whole crew from our class escorted us to a snowy embankment for the showdown. At that age I was not yet as big as my classmates or my opponent and hence I was the underdog. I did not want to do it but thought if I had to, I may as well be plucky and go all out. I won the fight and then summarily carried off on the shoulders of my classmates. In grade five I had another skirmish of a different kind. A pretty blonde girl and I were play wrestling on the school lawn when amidst the tussle her gold necklace broke. The next day our teacher called us outside of the classroom. She explained our horsing around required the girl's necklace to be repaired for $6 and that I should apologize to her. I felt badly that the chain broke however I also felt the request for an apology was unjust since the fault was equally hers as it was mine. This scuffle with the girl took place at St. Francis of Borsia, an English-speaking primary school that was situated right beside a French-speaking primary school, St. Catherine de Seine. In Montreal during the winter there were no shortage of snowstorms, and there were snowball fights between the two schools would often break out at recess; the students enjoyed it immensely. An Anglophone student at the French school, Bruce, who commuted with me on the school bus, invited me over for macaroni and cheese and we remained friends since then with variations on our diet that were no healthier but just as enjoyable for the longest time.

My parents believed strongly in a quality education and enrolled me into Loyola High School, a boy's private preparatory school in Montreal. I loved the established Edwardian architecture that is reminiscent of *Dead Poet's Society*, one of my favourite films. I walked 1.6 kilometers to my school and back to where I lived in Montreal West. Along the walk there was an unusually tame and friendly squirrel that would not only greet me but also run up my arm. This was a delight for the months I saw him, until he was gone.

Loyola excelled in academics and sports, although I was not a great student due to being hyperactive. I did enjoy the school, my close friends, and participated in multiple sports including hockey, as well as and being a member of the swim team. I still maintain friendships from those high school years. It was during my final years at Loyola that I started to see that the world was open to unlimited possibilities. Although I was driven, I was not yet effective in focusing my energies. I tended to be spread them out through time spent with my friends, the various sports I was involved with, artistic creations, and in grade 10 with my girlfriend, who was going to Trafalgar, a girl's-only academy. In high school I completed my Bronze Medallion lifeguarding certificate and was also on a winning swim team. I had a chance to see my swimming photo on the wall at my high school years later.

In the dead of winter my friends and I would go to the indoor hockey rink that was associated with the school and play on free ice time before classes for the day. In retrospect this was a real luxury by contrast to today's tapped out school budgets. The academic rigour of the school was a force not to be taking lightly. Not being the best listener, I was not at my prime for academics, but I did work hard, and thus graduated on schedule. An especially devoted physics teacher, Dr. Nish Mukerji, who was always available for students after hours had a tragic end being on-board the Air India flight 182 that was bombed in 1985. Going to an all-boys' school meant that contact with girls came mostly from dances with the other private girls' schools in the area: Sacred Heart, Queen of Angels and the Villa.

My time at high school was mostly good but my parents' separation meant this was a difficult time especially for my mother who had to make do in light of the circumstances. Although I found it hard to sit still, I was motivated to do the best I could, knowing from my parents the importance of a good education.

On my 40th anniversary of graduating from Loyola I organized a West Coast gathering for fellow graduates on the Pacific Rim with attendees from the West Coast, Mainland China and Hong Kong.

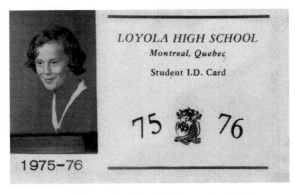

Loyola High School, Montreal, 1976

During post-secondary years I completed my one and only triathlon in 1981. These were the very early days of this sport. The race took place at the Montreal Olympic Stadium with swimming in the fabulous pools, running on an outdoor track, and finally bicycling in the Velodrome, the Olympic indoor cycling venue that years later was changed to become the Montreal Biodome. Four decades later I still run regularly, swim at our cottage; though rarely bike since we live on a very hilly island not conducive for road bikes. Many years later I ended up getting to know Les McDonald in Vancouver who had brought triathlon to Canada. He was a very astute head of the ITU (International Triathlon Union) and considering his position; he was always available to chat. Although we were not of the same political leanings, I enjoyed his constant questioning to see what and how much I knew.

He made a comment to me about meetings in international sport where he said to speak not of sport but of the politics of the country you are in. This way you will know what is going on and how things worked in that country. I attended his 80th birthday celebration and he passed away three years later.

With Les McDonald at his 80th birthday party. He brought Triathlon to Canada, North Vancouver, 2013

After high school, I focused on completing an advanced education as I felt that this was important before tackling a career. Before attending university, I completed a Pure and Applied Science diploma at Vanier College where the toughest course, the one I most rigorously worked at in my life was Calculus III. The first two Calculus courses were required and the third one was optional. The level III class started with 21 students; seven dropped it leaving 14. Of these, seven failed, and I was among the seven who passed. It was the hardest pass I had ever worked for. The teacher from Vietnam was very knowledgeable and demanding but her English was difficult to understand. Only one student received a top grade in the '80s, a laid-back Rastafarian, with a multi-coloured Jamaican hat, who was obviously a math genius.

During a summer break in 1981 I travelled with my friend Steffen to Calgary and worked for a valve repair company that serviced the natural gas industry. We had to take apart the valves, sand them down, then refurbish and paint them. It was hard work but it paid well which allowed us to leave on a road trip to California before going back home to Montreal. I returned home and took on a lifeguarding job at Westmount Park for the rest of the summer. At a young age I appreciated that being certified for positions like in lifeguarding would allow me to take on more interesting skilled jobs.

I explored engineering as a course of study but ended up taking commerce, which gave a good foundation to pursue many career options. There was one problem though; being accepted into a business program at Concordia University required an "A" average that I did not have. I looked at other faculties that I could get into, and they included arts. I entered university under a BA program and took some courses, but I was not convinced this would lead me to a wide option of career choices. I thought about it and decided to take the commerce courses anyway, even though I was not in the program. This was not easy, since at registration time I had to pick up any leftover spots from the commerce students if there were any available. I took the risk of pursuing this course of study for two years while still not being accepted in the faculty. I then requested a meeting with the assistant to the Dean of Commerce, Carol, and the meeting went like this:

Peter: "Thank you for seeing me today as I have a special request."

Carol: "I see. All requests are special."

Peter: "Yes, I understand. What may be unique in why I requested the meeting is that I have completed two years of the commerce program and I am asking to officially be admitted so I may complete my final year and my degree."

Carol: "This is highly unusual. I will have to look into this and I will let you know. It was great to meet you."

Peter: "Thank you, I appreciate your time."

A letter arrived shortly after stating that I was admitted into the program and my completed courses were now part of the commerce curriculum. Then a professor from the university called me to ask how I achieved this since nobody else had done this. With some help from Carol, I completed the B. Comm. with a major in Data Processing, and I returned the favour years later with some fundraising for the university.

Without any break after graduation I accepted an offer to work at Canadian Pacific in the Computers and Communications division. Not having another immediate option, I decided to take the job even though I had to move to Toronto for it. At the time, living in a new city was an adventure and I started work there right after graduation. After two years I asked for a leave for the summer as I felt I needed one after many years of study without a rest. I wanted the opportunity to clarify my career path. I also wanted to be in nature while I planned my next steps. I thought about what would be the ideal summer experience and I decided it should be a combination of 1. Outdoors, 2. Physical, and 3. Social. This combination is relatively rare. I decided that a white-water rafting guide would be the best combination in light that I was already a lifeguard, and so, it was not too much of a jump to be a guide. My friend Bruce and I drove out west, and he took on a job at the Athabasca Hotel while I accepted an offer to be a guide at White-Water Rafting Jasper.

After this fabulous summer I went back to my job in Toronto and worked until February 1988 when another interesting opportunity presented itself. I applied to volunteer for the Calgary Olympic Games and was given a spot in the media centre. I decided I wanted to contribute to these games after watching the 1984 Sarajevo Winter Olympics on television and seeing the Canadian flag at the closing ceremonies being raised, signaling that the next winter games were to be in Calgary. I felt this movement was something that celebrates human achievements and brings cultures together instead of dividing them, and I wanted to be part of it. I had no more vacation time left and again asked for a leave, this time for two weeks to travel to Calgary. The request was denied, and I decided to resign so I would not miss the opportunity. I am glad that I did since it proved to be a life changing experience to be part of something so grand. An executive in the company approached and said he would do the same if he were my age. Being invited to the athletes' party was a highlight. During the celebration, K.D. Lang sang, while I stood with a group of American athletes on my left who were dressed very casually in jeans and being social. On my right stood a group of group of reserved Soviet athletes dressed formally in somber grey suits and black skinny ties. One of the American male athletes reached out his arm in front of me to a Soviet male athlete and said; "We are all good friends, right?" This being during the Cold War was a moving sentiment. The Soviet athlete shook his hand and replied, "Yes, yes." It was a good reminder of why I was volunteering.

Not having a job to go back to, I returned to Montreal and rented an apartment on McGill campus for the summer while I looked for a new opportunity. It is here while living alone, a rare occurrence in my life, when I had the time to reflect on what would later become HEROISMS. I started a journal inspired by Prime Minister Mackenzie King of Canada who had done the same as he "Did not want to waste a day." I took on two jobs that summer. I was able to get my career back on track in office automation for General Electric in the Dominion Engineering division, later called GE Hydro and since then renamed GE Renewable Energy. The interview process required me to meet a French-Canadian human resources employee who had to follow the rules of the "Office Québécois de la Langue Française." Her job was to ensure French language proficiency in the workplace. I am able to speak French socially but was concerned whether it would be good enough for a professional workplace environment. I found out that I met her requirements. Later outside of work at a golf event she whispered in my ear to "Speak English to me." Clearly the rules of what language we should speak in Québec were different outside of the workplace.

The second job I took was for working on weekends where I rafted the Rivière Rouge near Montebello, Québec for New World River Expeditions. It was exhausting to do both jobs but I was single and rafting was a great way to spend the weekends for another summer. Working seven days a week had a downside though as one day driving back home late at night from rafting, I felt myself falling asleep at the wheel. I jolted myself twice back to consciousness and decided not to risk a third time and I pulled over at a truck stop near the town of Hudson and slept in the back of my Subaru wagon to not risk an accident. It was one of the wiser decisions I made in my life.

The quality of my life improved significantly being back in Montreal. I was able to buy my first house on a leafy country-like street in 1988 at 58 Waverley Rd., in Pointe-Claire South for $91,000, one of the items on my 100 Life Visions. I was also close to my parents, friends, and the family cottage in Vermont.

By returning to Montreal I had a lower cost of living compared to when I was in Toronto. To top this off in March of 1989 I met lovely Geraldine, the wonderful woman I would marry just a year later. She was at attending a party my friend Bruce was having and he was dating Geraldine's best friend, Gillian. Geraldine and I went to the same university and we would cross paths four times before I was introduced to her that night. After meeting we felt an immediate connection and found out we lived only a few blocks from each other in Pointe-Claire. I read that most people marry someone who lives within 1.6 km. In today's globalized world I thought this might not apply anymore, but it did for us too. One of the first courtships I took Geraldine on was white-water rafting where I was her guide. Soon after Bruce, Gillian, Geraldine and I had great times together as two couples going to each of our family's cottages, either near Stowe, Vermont, or Bark Lake in the Laurentians north of Montreal. It is not often that you have a close friendship between two couples where everyone is in-sync. If you have one or more of these relationships then you are fortunate.

Taking out a Laser with Bruce, Bark Lake, 1987

My modus operandi is for my existence to be broad in scope, and meaningful. Many things captured my imagination so I had the advantage of never being bored, but at the same time made it more of a challenge to focus. Before I met Geraldine, I had decided to pursue graduate school and to explore the connection between computer technology and building architecture. I applied to the University of Colorado for the fall of 1989. Initially I was not accepted, but I called the dean and gave my argument for why they may wish to reconsider. It worked, and I was accepted into their graduate program.

Do not take 'no' for an answer. If you cannot find a solution it does not mean the solution is not there; it just means you are not being creative enough to find it. Keep looking.

It was early in my relationship with Geraldine, which led us to the decision that we would live apart while I attended the first semester and we would take it from there. I gave up a solid career that I enjoyed at GE and I drove to Colorado. My house was left rented and off I went. The experience was excellent although financially it was unsustainable at the time. On top of this, living apart was something we wanted to resolve. We decided that I would go back to Montreal and we could plan our new life direction when I was there. When I came back at Christmas I proposed to Geraldine and we married in the summer of 1990. Since we lived in Pointe-Claire and were residents of this municipality, we were able to book Stewart Hall, a beautiful waterfront stone mansion, for the wedding reception. With a modest budget of $5,000 and Geraldine's mother Lori coordinating the catering and acting as head chef, we had a wonderful wedding on a hot July day with 75 guests in attendance.

At our wedding reception, Stuart Hall, Pointe-Claire, 1990

I found Computer Assisted Design (CAD) work at Air Canada and I did this for a year before Geraldine decided she wanted to leave her technical writing job and pursue a career in teaching. She applied and was accepted at UBC in Vancouver. We were still in our late 20s when we loaded up a truck with a trailer and drove out to Vancouver.

In 1991 Vancouver was booming and there was a significant shortage of rental accommodation in the city especially for anyone having a dog. We found a rare apartment that allowed animals at 1629 Haro St., and living there was like being in a zoo as there were all

Geraldine and I, Montreal, 1991

kinds of critters coming in and out of the elevator. I found work again in CAD and took more architecture courses.

We narrowed down our choices on where to settle, either on Bowen Island or White Rock. We visited both towns and walked a picturesque trail around Killarney Lake on Bowen Island. On another trip to the island Geraldine met the principal at the Bowen Island Community School which is part of the West Vancouver School District. When Geraldine finished her studies at UBC, the faculty told the graduating students not to bother applying to the West Vancouver School District since they hire from their teacher on call list. Geraldine arranged to have her name placed on this list and she was hired for a one-day-a-week position that kept increasing until she was eventually working full-time. This is an example in life where half of the success in life is showing up.

We rented a home on Bowen Island that did not have central heating for half of the house, and we needed to stoke a wood-burning fireplace to stay warm in the winter. We were not able to buy a house yet so we rented for the first six years while living on the island.

The CAD work transitioned to a sales role in the same industry that taught me protocols in how to attract clients and business opportunities. My original vision of merging computers and architecture as a career did not materialize the way I envisioned, and so I decided that the best plan was for me was to capitalize on my strengths of having my business degree and now some relevant experience, and I looked at getting back to what I considered doing first in my career, namely in the investment industry.

Before making a move to investments I was invited to be on an accreditation team to evaluate one of University of Notre Dame's colleges. I flew to South Bend, Indiana and walked the fabulous campus adorned with beautiful gothic architecture. I went for a swim under memorable towering stone arches. The accreditation team was invited to the dean of architecture's home, which was a contemporary-built Roman villa. Everything from the painted wall frescoes, flowing cloth from the ceiling, and Roman-inspired antique furniture and architecture made it a very interesting and enjoyable evening. An inspirational film Rudy, based on a true story of a student at Notre Dame, was filmed at this campus, so it was great to see the sites up close and in person.

My entry into wealth management was preceded by a full year of research before making a move, and I interviewed or was interviewed by 20 people before I made a well-informed decision on how the industry functioned, and thus joined ScotiaMcLeod at a new office in West Vancouver. This was a good move, and I worked the hardest in my life on developing my clientele since failure was not an option with our first daughter Francesca just a few months old when I joined the firm.

> *Take the time to know what you want to pursue, and then take control of that vision like a laser beam.*

Francesca was born in 1996, the year I took courses to prepare for my new career of being an investment advisor. Selena our second daughter was born in 1999 and at the point our rental home was no longer large enough for our family of four. Fortunately, my work propelled forward and we were able to support a mortgage on a home we purchased for $231,000. The house was modest but charming, and worked very well for our new family. The backyard tree house, swing, and garden were great for the young girls. The purchase was good timing since within two years of buying, prices started to move up significantly in the Greater Vancouver Regional District. In 2005 we moved to a new home, also on the island, and we have lived there ever since.

Our second home on Bowen Island since 2005

By the year 2000, in my third year in the investment profession, I had developed solid client relationships and had the critical mass to survive in the business. The education offered by the firm was very good as they had extensive rookie programs in those days that are now much fewer. Firms are now mostly focused on hiring experienced advisors with their client base from other firms instead of developing new recruits. Outside of the large firms in the investment industry it is rare to be able to get hired as a rookie, be paid a salary to develop a clientele that you can eventually transition to your successor when you retire and earn a solid income. There is under this arrangement a unique combination of entrepreneurialism while offering stability until you reach critical mass. There is creativity, freedom, constant learning, and social interaction that suited me very well for these aspects of the profession. However, the endless paperwork and rules to follow can be burdensome but you adjust to these realities. Other interests like owning a cottage on a lake remained but were relegated to the back burner. Since I did not pursue computers and architecture any further, I still had to achieve the life goal of being involved in designing and building a home. I accomplished this in 2014 by building a 2,800 sq. ft. cottage on lakefront acreage.

The sooner you know your path the better. The 20s allow for experimenting, but by the early 30s it is best to have focus.

With my career as a financial advisor now four years old, business development became a major focus. I was working out of a new, elegant West Vancouver office and bringing on clients through a number of different ways. After some false starts, the strategy that worked enough to get going was calling the graduates from my alma mater. I learned later on that focusing on retiring advisors could be a highly effective approach to build your client base as instead of bringing on one client at a time, you can take on an entire book of relationships.

In the later part of my career I was able to make three deals with retiring advisors leaving the business. This came from a focused effort to get to know advisors who were planning to retire. The other thing that worked well was networking and meeting people in my normal daily life, whether it was at a gym, waiting for a ferry, and social gatherings.

The next ten years moved me to the head office of ScotiaMcLeod in downtown Vancouver. I focused on giving seminar presentations titled, "Six Investment Models™ and 'The Art of War' by Sun Tzu." I gave more than 60 seminars and it worked in the sense that I had established a finely-honed presentation, which was repeatable and therefore efficient to deliver. The challenge was to ensure that enough attendees came to have critical mass, the ideal being 8-12 people. I was initially apprehensive of moving downtown as I enjoyed a running group that ran out of the West Vancouver Recreation Centre and the area was a beautiful and relatively calm place to work. However, once downtown I enjoyed the contrast of the activity of working in the city and the lifestyle of living on an island.

After fifteen years in 2012 I changed firms where I became a partner of an independent office of Raymond James. Moving clients can be a very stressful exercise and poor planning may destroy your career. I prepared for five months and I made a list of the possible things that could go wrong. Each on its own had a low chance of occurrence; however, there were many moving parts, and when added up the odds of something going sideways was 40%. I included events such as: accidents, sickness, natural disasters, and pandemics. I was especially careful with my diet, as well as driving during this time. I found that it was very effective to hire a chauffeur and be driven from client to client wherever I could get a meeting. This way, instead of driving, I could focus on speaking with my clients, making phone calls and confirming appointments. After one month most of the important work towards bringing on your clients is complete.

What made this transition especially stressful is that the regulatory rules do not allow disclosing that you are changing firms until you have resigned from the old firm and you are registered with a new one. I followed the rules, which meant clients I called were sometimes shocked to hear the news since I was not able to given them a warning.

When planning a challenge to your environment the benefits of the change must be significant enough to offset the risk of undertaking the change.

The offer I received was to be a partner in a relatively new office of Raymond James, and therefore, hold ownership and an equal vote on business protocol. This was unique enough to warrant the risks of change. It was also apparent at my former firm that they would be changing their business model, which could lead to downsizing. This did happen and four years after I left, 67 advisors were let go across Canada. Since they were given no notice they had to scramble, mostly unprepared, to find a new firm to work for. In our office we were able to hire three of these advisors.

CHAPTER TWO

100 LIFE VISIONS

B efore tackling HEROISMS, a good first step is to create a grand life plan in a table with four columns: Number, Category, Goal, and Date of Achievement, either electronically or in a handwritten system. The categories may be broken down into the main elements of life, HEROISMS:

Health

Education

Relations (family, friends)

Occupation (work, career)

Interests (sports, music, writing, art, travel, etc.)

Society (volunteering, community involvement, charities)

Money (personal finance and investing)

Spirituality

Begin by reflecting on what you have already accomplished to date in your life in each of these categories. Going back year over year helps you chronologically review your record. Once this is ready, look at each of the categories above and think what you would like to accomplish without restriction. Do not let any preconceived thoughts or financial restrictions limit your creative ideas. Write out your grand vision, as well as the steps to get there that may be worked on later. The more precise your vision the better and the more likely you will be able to achieve your goals. The list should not only be precise but also measurable. If you only write "travel," it is too vague, but if you write that your vision is to "take my parents to Hawaii to snorkel with sea turtles on their 50th anniversary," then it is a clear objective and you will know if you have met that goal. Do not be afraid to write grand visions or dreams that may seem overwhelming at first appearance, e.g. learn two more languages. The interim steps to achieve the grand designs may be part of the annual list of goals. Do not be surprised if you have difficulty coming up with 100 items, as this requires reflection, creativity, and often some time spanning well beyond one planning session. The list may be open to changes, additions, and deletions as the years pass, and goals that once seemed worthy of pursuit may no longer be deemed important, and likewise new ideas and unexpected opportunities will lead to new avenues that you wish to pursue.

The annual list is the next thing to tackle. Since there are twelve months in a year, I suggest 10 goals, one for each month and two free months as a workable target. Of the 10 goals a minimum of two should be taken from your 100 Life Visions, and the remaining eight goals should be objectives that are lesser in the scale of difficulty but things you wish still to achieve in the year, e.g. a renovation of a room in your house, volunteering on a community project, writing an article in the local paper, or a family vacation. If you choose only one life goal to tackle for the year it is unlikely you will finish 100 Life Visions unless you live well past 100 and in good health! Attempting more than three may be too onerous if you have normal life commitments of family, career, or education. Take ample time to make the annual list, one that is written down, possibly in a journal, and one you can review periodically throughout the year, and especially at year-end. Once a year has passed and you reflect back on your goals, mark yourself on how you have done. A critical, honest evaluation allows for improvement for the following year. If you completed eight of the 10 goals, first congratulate yourself for the ones completed, and think about the two you did not. Should one or more of the two be carried forward to the next year, or are they no longer important in favour of new and more worthy pursuits?

SEASONALITY OF LIFE

There is seasonality in nature, investing, and in life where you may divide spring, summer, fall, and winter into multiple year increments. Each circle below represents one month, and since the average person lives to 82 there may only be 84 months in winter.

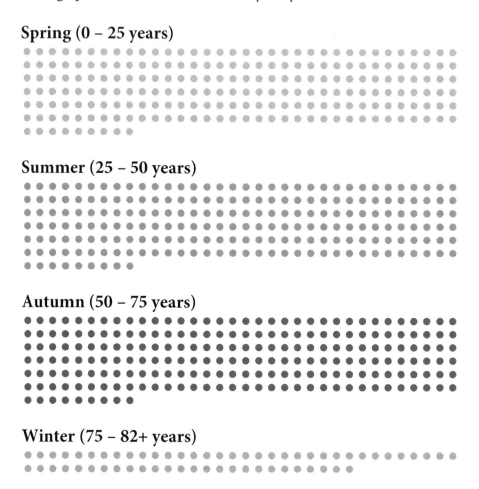

Spring (0 – 25 years)

Summer (25 – 50 years)

Autumn (50 – 75 years)

Winter (75 – 82+ years)

There is no time to waste, so focus on what is important.

8 PILLARS OF HEROISMS

"People say that what we're seeking is a meaning for life. I think what we're really seeking is an experience of being alive, so that our life experiences on the purely physical plane will have resonances with our innermost being and reality, so that we can actually feel the rapture of being alive."

Joseph Campbell

CHAPTER THREE

HEALTH – THE FIRST WEALTH

Medical

"The part can never be well unless the whole is well."

Plato

What is more important than having an overview of your health? Very little. You may be more likely to understand how your car works than knowing the inner workings of your body. You know when to service your vehicle but may not know when to have a prostrate exam or, to test to check the condition of your arteries. To address this need you, need a service record - for you.

I created a worksheet that records health details for over the course of your lifetime. I put my health records in a binder with important historical details that may be useful for medical professionals. When I go to a doctor, I bring the binder and I can give him or her a copy of this record for details he may wish to see. The general feedback from doctors is that they are impressed as they have never seen this before and they wish other patients would do the same. I have noticed that systems have improved at doctors' offices and they now have sophisticated computerized record keeping that link with multiple specialties. Your own records are still useful for longer-term data and for visiting medical professionals who do not have your long-term history. See Appendix B.

In the spring of 2009, I noticed that my time on my regular 5.5 km trail run around Killarney Lake, near where I live, was slowing down. Then one day I could not finish my run and had to walk back the last kilometer, something that had never before happened. I put this down to being overworked and so I took a couple of days off from my running. After this rest I headed out on the trails and after two minutes of running dizziness came over me so powerfully that if I had not sat down on the trail I would have fallen over. I walked home realizing that there was something seriously wrong. The best way I can describe the feeling was one of having a performance car but bogged down with a clogged fuel filter. No matter how powerful the engine, it is limited by the amount of fuel intake. I called Doug an Olympian doctor I knew and he asked me questions for half an hour. Afterwards he said, "What you have is serious and you have to go have it checked out immediately." I set an appointment with a cardiologist I knew, who was old school and surprising for a doctor today, a smoker. He arranged for me to run on a treadmill, and in the interim, injected me with a nuclear dye. After analyzing the data, he thought that I had some lesser arterial blockages that could be treated with medication, surgery not being necessary. He prescribed pills that I later found were out of date in place of more contemporary medication. He did say that I could have an angiogram to get a more accurate picture, but it was not required. Going home on that sunny July day I reflected on how dramatically my running capacity had slowed down and that I did not want to take any chances, and so I went ahead and requested an angiogram. The appointment was set for December 2009, five months away. In the meantime, I felt good, but I felt I had a blockage of some kind, which is exactly what I had. On the day of the angiogram a cardiologist performed a test that consists of inserting a wire from the groin and into the arteries, providing a clear picture of any blockages. After the procedure he came over to me and with real surprise said, "What are you doing here? You are lean, and you are a runner; you should not be here." He continued, "You have major artery blockages with some at 100%. We will need to do an angioplasty right away." Fortunately, I caught this before a potential heart attack!

I attribute the cause to three factors: genetics, stress, and too many French fries in high school. I learned how dangerous stress could be to one's health. After reading about nutrition I realized my diet was okay, but not as good as I thought. I went from good to very good but there was still room for improvement. According to my reading the only known way to reverse heart artery blockages is a plant-based diet. I did a follow-up on the angioplasty in 2019 with a less invasive procedure using a CT scan and the good news was that I did not have material blockages anymore. Even partial is not good enough for me so I implemented a primarily plant-based diet. I intentionally did not want the stress of going 100% as I think what you do the vast majority of the time is important and not the occasional diversion.

Do your own homework when it comes to your health to augment the professional help from your doctor.

The first hint that I may have had some artery restrictions came when I went for a run with my Karate club in Toronto in 1987. I noticed I was giving it everything I had while some other karate students were running at my pace with what seemed like little effort. I thought this was simply due to some people being naturally better runners than others. Interestingly, martial arts require explosive, fast action and I had no restrictions there. It would be 22 years later in 2009 when the artery clogging came to roost. So how did I manage so well in the interim? I attribute this to partially clogged arteries when I was 25 and I managed to do everything I wanted, as it was not a dire issue at the time. When the blockages became serious then it was a different story. In 1999 I had a cholesterol test and the doctor at the time said my level was normal, but high normal and he had left it at that. What I know now is that 'normal' is normal to the average Joe who does not have an optimal health situation. The right advice for me at the time would have been to give a serious warning to study an optimal diet and bring my cholesterol down to much lower levels. Ten years later the problem arose.

Fitness

I always enjoyed exercise, sports, and especially being outdoors. Swimming was the first organized sport I was intensely involved in. I was part of the Montreal West swim club in the summers and during the school year I was on my high school swim team. The workouts were grueling and we competed at multiple pools across the West Island of Montreal. I was not a first seeded swimmer, although I still enjoyed the challenge and this set the stage for other water activities, including being a lifeguard and a white-water rafting guide.

In early high school, a friend of mine Kevin, had a gym set with plastic-encased concrete weights and a bench. I tried it but it was not until university that I embraced working out as part of my fitness routine. I decided to wait until I ran a marathon before starting weights. As soon as I completed the race, I ended long distance running and started a gym routine. My university's weight room was basic but adequate at the aging athletic complex at the time. It was here that I noticed that I had a longer torso than many people since I had to adjust down a bench on a pull-down bar. Before then I do not think I had ever noticed this. I quickly benefited from the early gains of picking up weight training and my personal record of benching 205 lbs. At the time I would have weighed 155 lbs. After university I worked as a consultant at Air Canada where there was a gym that provided me the opportunity to work out at lunch, a routine I still maintain today. Working out in the morning was not my favourite way to start the day, and in the evening life often intervened. By using my lunch hour to work out and then eat at my desk worked like a charm. Thirty years later

I maintain my lunch hour workout routine whether it be at a gym, trail running, or yoga.

Yoga was something I tried later on but did not become part of my schedule until I was 56 when I realized that as you age, it was a wise activity to pick up for stretching. On my own I would rarely stretch more than briefly, but yoga disciplines you to stretch for an hour at every class. I tried a form of extreme yoga in 2010 by watching a video and I damaged my shoulder, which took a long time to recover. The movement was an upside-down arch and when I extended my arms, I felt a tear in my muscles. The video did say that this was an advanced move! Ironically, I picked up yoga to prevent injury rather than experiencing it. Now I go to a class with seasoned instructors and I do not have any injuries.

Nutrition

In my teens and my early twenties, I had an awful diet when away from home but so did my friends. Hot dogs, hamburgers, and French fries were a daily staple in the '70s and at the time, I loved it. I started to learn about nutrition in university and began to make better choices by dropping processed meats, and eating more salads. Overall, I still did not have a healthy diet, but I was lean since I was active and lived on my bicycle. When I look back at the insanity of eating in a way that may clogs your arteries, I cringe.

To optimize a healthier way of eating, construct a reference sheet for what you should do, limit, and avoid.

CHAPTER FOUR

EDUCATION – LIFE-LONG LEARNING

"Live as if you were to die tomorrow. Learn as if you were to live forever."

Gandhi

College

In Québec, high school is followed by CEGEP, a two-year diploma that is a usually a precursor to attending university. I enrolled at Vanier College in their most rigorous program, Pure and Applied Sciences. I was an average student at best, but if there is one quality I possessed throughout my education and life it is persistence. I could have entered university as a mature student by working a couple of years and in my circumstances, it may have been a better avenue to pursue, since I did not have the grades for scholarships, and I could have solidified my personal finances before attending university on more solid financial footing.

Persistence more than any other quality is needed to achieve success in whatever you pursue.

Undergraduate

I followed up college by attending Concordia University in Montreal at a campus that was shared by Loyola High School where I had also attended. The other campus was situated in the centre of the city, though it was more of an office-type building and lacked the charm of the leafy, established Loyola campus. I would fight to get my courses at Loyola whenever possible.

A system I use to this day was one I had developed in university. I would aim to have all of my courses span from Monday to Thursday. Thursday night was my night to socialize at the campus centre and Friday to Sunday were study days. Today I still prefer to have any social events on Thursday nights that are then followed by working out of my home office on Fridays. Although I work on Fridays, it is a nice transition to the weekend being at home, and after work I head out into the forest trails for my 5.5 km run, a ritual I have kept since we moved to Bowen Island in 1993. I first tested working at home on Fridays in the year 2000. There was an immediate 20% increase in the quality of my life. I have not looked back.

Look for ways that work and once you find them, embrace them.

In my second to last semester at Concordia I was anxious over the difficult financial situation I found myself as a student, and I considered getting a full-time job and finishing my degree part-time. I went for an interview and the interviewer said, "You have a good résumé so make sure you finish your degree first." I took the advice and focused my energy on getting through the last two semesters before working.

Graduate

After my B. Comm. I pursued more courses at the graduate level at the University of Colorado, Denver, as I was interested in the interrelationship of computers and architecture. I enjoyed the experience but my foray into this profession did not lead to where I wanted. I then leveraged off of my business degree and pursued a career in portfolio management obtaining a professional designation in financial planning (CFP), and I completed numerous courses related to finance. With serious consideration of getting an MBA, I called Dalhousie University since they had a remote education program designed for investment professionals. I phoned the admissions office and the administrator said they had a strict cut-off on grade point averages for acceptance. I just missed the cut off, and she said not to apply due to this hard and fast rule. I took this as a challenge and I proceeded to create what I thought would be an outstanding application. It worked, and although I was accepted into their MBA program, I lost interest because focusing on my clients and building on the foundation I had built in my wealth management practice was a better choice at the time. Advanced education is a good idea but the timing was not right. I enjoy learning and continually look for ways to expand my horizons, e.g. public speaking, most notably when I was a speaker at TEDx Abbotsford in 2019.

Professional

There are endless courses to take within the investment profession. In my jurisdiction the basic requirements are normally a university degree, the Canadian Securities Course and an ethics course. It is a common practice to pursue a CFP (Chartered Financial Planner), an MBA (Masters of Business Administration) or CFA (Chartered Financial Analyst). The general consensus is that the CFA is the most difficult program to complete and allows for the most options in the investment industry. In the financial world there are numerous specialties including portfolio management, options or futures licensing, insurance, and financial planning. On top of this there are continuing education and compliance courses you can take to maintain your licensing. Courses and coaching also exist to bring someone to another level in their professional and personal lives.

The industry specific memberships and accreditations come with not only letters but with annual bills that will last a career. You should be careful which and how many designations you pursue as some are beneficial and others are less so. Unlike a university degree that once granted carries no more costs except for voluntary donations to annual alma mater fundraising campaigns.

There are various specialties within the financial services industry where the main difference between a financial advisor and a portfolio manager is that a portfolio manager has discretionary authority to manage a portfolio for a client without needing approval for every transaction.

Education is one piece of the puzzle of competence but not the main driver for success in building a book of clients. On top of learning, you must be able demonstrate to a potential client that: 1. They know who you are, because if a potential client never knows who the advisor is, how will the advisor, no matter how brilliant, be able to bring on a client; 2. The advisor has a personality that resonates with potential clients; and 3. The potential client may trust the advisor to be competent in his wealth management capacities.

I attended a dinner event at the Jonathan Club in Los Angeles in 2002 where I met an assistant to an advisor who had both his CFA and MBA. He said he could not get a client if his life depended on it, but he felt he had solid analytic skills that were well used for an advisor he worked for. On the other end of the spectrum I have seen great success for advisors who have had a normal education but clearly had the critical qualities of being hard working and persistent. Of the many qualities needed, persistence is the most important towards achieving success as long as it is in the context of having a solid character. Ideally, a degree from a reputable university, along with character, and a track record of success in business offers the most solid foundation. The key is to know your strengths and delegate your weaknesses. There is a mentor of mine is very scientifically minded and spends much of his time scrutinizing and testing investment models; he rarely speaks to clients and yet he has built a very strong practice. He knows client servicing is not his strength and he delegates a team to take care of the clients while he has the time to pursue his analytical capacities.

Perhaps the most practical education comes from experience and personal initiatives, learning from colleagues, and targeted reading. An effective learning approach would be to identify a recognized expert in the field of work you wish to pursue. If you can gain a position in this type of environment that would be one avenue; although, an accelerated approach would be to ask if you could be a fly on the wall in the right person's office for one week. You would do nothing else but listen to the goings on and observe and take notes. This education could be worth its weight in gold and can leapfrog your career. Early in my career I managed to identify whom this person would be as he demonstrated a type of systemized, rules-based approach I sought. I was discouraged from reaching out to this advisor as he is very private, but I eventually met him at a conference in Banff, Alberta, and then 11 years after this we reconnected and we maintain contact through email. I could have accelerated my systems by a decade if I would have learned back then what I know now.

"My strength lies solely in my tenacity."

Louis Pasteur

CHAPTER FIVE

RELATIONS – FAMILY AND FRIENDS

"Women select men. That makes them nature, because nature is what selects. … The woman is the gatekeeper to reproductive success, and you can't get more like nature than that, in fact it's the very definition of nature."

Jordan B. Peterson

Bachelor

I think of 16 as the age when I began having relationships with women, for a total of 10 years before I met lovely Geraldine and married soon after. When I ask people how many times they were in love in their lives, the answers range from zero to five with the average being two. The surprising outcome of this informal survey was the amount of time I heard 'zero.' Why is it that humanity with an average of 82 years on this earth with countless human interactions has experienced so few loving relationships? Whatever the reason, it is good to be aware of this phenomenon, and if you are fortunate to be in a deep relationship then you should be aware of how precious it is.

For two summers I went to "Base de Plein Air" a summer camp in the Laurentians near St. Jovite, Québec where I gave my first relationship advice. The most beautiful girl in the camp was a striking 16-year-old Russian who moved to Canada and who told me that she played a card game that would indicate to her which of two boys at the camp was right for her. She said that the cards had read me as the right choice. At that young age I was not one to miss out on life opportunities, especially ones as good as this, and I accepted the game result and the chance to get to know her for the rest of the time at camp.

My first lesson about women began here, namely that they often make decisions primarily on feelings and intuition of the moment. After this fortuitous event another male camper asked if he could speak to me in private. We sat down, each on his own bunk bed, and he wanted advice on how to get a girl like the one I had. With limited experience to draw on I still tried to help, and I shared my thought that in effect, it was to be attractive in some way. I give full credit to this other young camper for reflecting on how to achieve your goals, putting ego aside and not being afraid to ask. With this attitude I bet he went on to be successful in life.

Summer camp was followed by visiting Bruce at his family's cottage at Bark Lake, also in the Laurentians. At his cottage, a boat pulled up to his dock and a pretty blonde girl and her younger brother who also had a place on the lake, stepped out of their boat. I was smitten by her beauty and lively personality, and she became what I considered to be my first girlfriend.

A few years later the next woman who had a real impact on me was in 1983 while I was in university and I took my first trip to Europe to visit relatives I had never met in Budapest.

Marathon training, Budapest, 1983

I flew to Vienna and then went to Westbanhof, the main train station and I sat beside two women from Germany who were going on holidays to Hungary. There was an instant connection with one of the women, Theresia and when we arrived in Budapest, I asked them to wait to see if my uncle would allow them to stay at his place. In retrospect since I had never even met my aunt, uncle nor cousins, I may have put my uncle on the spot; however, he agreed to have them, and all went well. The next day the women left for Lake Balaton and they agreed to come back in a few days. I was in Europe for many weeks and we saw the sights of the city together. We stayed in touch for years with trips to see each other in Canada, as well as skiing in Mayherhoffen, Austria. On her last trip to Canada, I knew that I was not in the right stage of my life to settle down and it was not fair for me to draw her into a life that was full of unknowns. We remained friends, and I was happy to see that she has her own family with two children in a beautiful Bavarian town.

I learned a lot when I was single about the nature of relationships. I came up with my own criteria that I think best describes the qualities many women look for in a partner that triggers attraction; security and physicality (S&P):

Security

Status (accomplishments)

Protection (ability to take care of partner)

Income

Physicality

Health

Attraction (one measurable quality is a wide shoulder to hip ratio, ideally 1.618 to 1, a golden ratio)

Height (the biological difference in height between men and woman is six inches so this may be the average height differential expected. What seems to be paramount in all but rare cases are for the man to be taller than the woman.

Strength

The security component for many women is there for all ages but minimal in youth, higher once out of the university age and paramount another decade later.

At a social event at the Terminal City Club in Vancouver I spoke with a doctor I knew and she volunteered that she was looking for a partner. I said, "Tell me what qualities you are looking for and I may be able to help." She replied, "He must be healthy since I am a doctor, fit and social." I thought about this and I recognized that there was something missing in her request. As an opportunity to test my theory I said, "I know someone who is not only healthy, he loves to cook meals with the freshest ingredients; he is not only fit but lean and muscular, and he is the life of a party." She said, "Fabulous, when can I meet him?" I carefully watched her reaction as I said, "I can arrange for you to meet since he works as a cashier at a clothing store in a nearby mall." She took one step back and said, "Peter, I do not want some guy working in a clothing store, I am a doctor. I want a multimillionaire!" What happened to her requirements? I described the person who had all the traits she asked for. To be healthy, fit, and social were important to her but only if the man first demonstrated the attributes of S&P!

A mature woman's primary requirement of security over physicality is the opposite for man's primary interest in physicality over security in a woman.

Understanding what potential partners look for is important to know, but how do you meet them? Today the online community has taken hold for the obvious reason that it is a highly effective sorting mechanism for introductions. You may set up meetings every day of the week all month long if you so wish.

A friend of mine called me to say that his marriage ended and he set up 10 dates for the next two weeks using online dating sites. He phoned back two weeks later to say that he "had the 10 dates and two were keepers." He chose one and he had his new partner. Very effective! What are other ways to meet potential partners? Since my dating days were before the Internet and social media took off, I found another highly effective way. For two summers I worked as a white-water rafting guide in both Alberta and Québec. As a guide, one of my jobs was to delegate and direct the guests that would come off busses and go to the awaiting rafts. On average a bus brought 40 guests, and normally one half were men and the other half women. If there were on average 20 female guests, then using my 5% rule would translate to my having a natural attraction for one of the female guests. While doing the security briefing, I would ensure the one woman that I pre-identified would be designated to my boat. The rafting that followed allowed an opportunity for my chosen guests to get to know me. After shooting the rapids, dinner and social activities would take place. This pattern would then repeat each day, and by the end of the summer, my address book would be overflowing.

Demonstrating S&P triggers overall attraction, and these qualities are most useful if there is a volume of potential partners to meet. I mentioned how rafting offered many social interactions but what other ways outside of the internet and rafting may this volume be found? The best is by demonstrating competence in a field where there is a significant level of social interaction, e.g. competitive sports, a guide for outdoors activities such as hiking, and horseback riding. If someone is not sport-oriented then other effective jobs include: fashion photographer, musician, resort entertainment staff, or art gallery host. By following these guidelines, the freedom of being single turns into a situation of how to choose a partner, if you wish among the volume of new connections:

1. Identify a system for a volume of social interactions

2. Execute the system

3. Demonstrate S&P

Family

Marriage – A Unity of Souls

Geraldine and I met on March 24, 1989, at my friend Bruce's house in Montreal West where he was having a party. She was 25 and I was 26. I was immediately smitten by Geraldine's beautiful smile and wanted to get to know her better. Interestingly I had a number of recollections of Geraldine before I met her. The first was in 1982 when I went to the humour pavilion at Man and His World, on the former site of Expo '67 in Montreal. Geraldine was 19 and a hostess there when I walked into the pavilion and saw her with her flowing blonde hair, wearing a hat, and her face pointing down so she did not notice me. I thought she was a very pretty, but she did not look very happy considering it was the "humour pavilion." I found out later that she was unhappy leaving her friends behind in Vienna where her father worked for the UN. Years later in 1985 I worked in my university's audiovisual department and I had to film a theater class. I focused my camera on a very pretty woman in the back of the class and I later found out that Geraldine was taking theatre classes there. A third recollection was when I was completing exams on an early summer evening. As I walked through the Guadangi Lounge at Concordia University, and I saw a lovely woman reading a book while fanning her white dress in the hot humid early summer night. I stopped and considered walking over to speak to her, but with me being in the middle of exams, I needed to focus on my next test and so I missed that opportunity. Next, I went to a volleyball game, also held at my university, to see if I would be interested in picking up the sport. I sat in the bleachers and a beautiful and friendly woman briefly spoke to me before we both went onto the court and played. I again found out later that this was Geraldine. I ended up choosing martial arts over volleyball. Four years later, a university friend, Jennifer and I decided to meet at Gertrude's, a student pub on McGill University's campus. I brought my friend Bruce and she brought her friend Gillian. Bruce and Gillian connected and became a couple.

Gillian is still one of Geraldine's best friends. Bruce and Gillian had a fateful party where Geraldine and I were introduced. After meeting Geraldine, I wanted to drive her home but I had had a few drinks so I did not. Early the next morning I left a single red rose at the front door of her house, which happened to be very close to mine in Pointe-Claire South, a suburb of Montreal. Unexpectedly, her father came out to get the newspaper and so I introduced myself and then left. After getting to know Geraldine, I suggested that we take a trip to Colorado since I was accepted into graduate studies. We had a great time travelling from San Francisco to Denver and back. I went ahead to study in Denver for one semester since I did not want to one day to look back and wonder what I had missed if I did not explore these studies. Financially, it pushed my resources to the limit to do only one semester, but I enjoyed the fresh experience, and Geraldine even came to visit and we would take trips to Aspen and Rocky Mountain National Park.

If Geraldine and I had not met I may have been resourceful enough to find ways to finance the rest of the Master's degree, but I decided to go back to Montreal and rethink my direction. I proposed to her very soon after and we made a commitment to each other, and at that point I had to get back on track with my career. The disruption of my studies and a lack of clear direction took years to resolve before I entered the investment industry, which put us on a solid financial footing and on a better path. This career choice was a good move since the profession made use of my interpersonal skills, mathematical aptitude, and entrepreneurial spirit.

In 1996, our first daughter, Francesca was born after a very difficult delivery of 33 hours. Francesca looked very much like me so there was no risk of mixing her up at the hospital. She came into our lives when I was 34 and studying to get into the investment industry. Selena joined us in 1999 and we hired a doula since Francesca's birth had been so difficult. Selena was born in one and half hours from start to finish. We were thankful we made it to the hospital from Bowen Island in time. Her delivery was easy in comparison to Francesca, and the doula may have witnessed one of the most efficient deliveries in her career. Selena was so quiet and calm that we had to check on her regularly to make sure she was okay. We were all living on the top floor of a rental home spanning 700 square feet. With the four of us living there now, we needed to move on and buy a house.

Parenthood

Growing up I felt that having at least two children would be ideal for a family. I thought that one girl and one boy, or two boys would be in my cards. In the end we had two delightful girls. Geraldine and I did discuss having a third

Geraldine and I, 2009

child but we ended up having two. Through my parenting I wanted to be part of whatever activities my daughters engaged in and this only happened to an extent. Mostly I was a driver where I was able to take them swimming, skiing, dancing, cheerleading, or horseback riding. As the girls grew into adults Francesca would join me on 5.5 km trail runs while Selena preferred to walk or go to the gym. I set out as a parent to teach by example, and this way I felt I could show my daughters what was possible through my reflections, as well as recording my goals every year and reviewing them. See Appendix A.

Geraldine's birthday at The Boathouse, West Vancouver, 2004

One the best gifts I gave to my girls were white boards, which allow for creativity, reflection, and planning. When the girls were three, I started an annual exercise of interviewing each girl on camera, which I did for 15 years. This was a big hit as our family is now able to look back and watch the kids' development and way of thinking over the years. The idea was inspired by a 1964 British documentary called *7 Up* where children were interviewed at age seven in the 1960's and every seven years thereafter. The series keeps getting updated and the last one is called *63 Up*, released in 2019.

In the girls' school district there was a contest to create an Olympic pin for the 2010 Olympic and Paralympic Games. Francesca was in the right grade to apply and I encouraged her to do this knowing that there would be a unique experience if she were to be connected to the games. She drew a great design and won the right to have her pin made for the games along with a few other students in the West Vancouver School District. The exposure gave her the chance to be introduced to the mayor of West Vancouver; who used to wear Francesca's pin. It was also a hit for me to see people on the street wearing her pin during the Olympics. During the games Francesca was offered a chance to be a reporter, and she wrote two articles for the <u>North Shore News</u>. To top it off, as a class project, her school made a life-size ceramic mosaic of her pin and it is permanently displayed on the exterior wall of the Bowen Island

Community School. During the Olympics and Paralympics Coca-Cola, an international Olympic sponsor, had a large display board where they collected thousands of pins. After the games, the board was shipped to the Coca-Cola museum in Atlanta, Georgia, and before it was shipped off, I took the opportunity to get on a chair and at the top middle of the board, I attached Francesca's pin so it would be easy to find if she ever visits Atlanta.

Since Geraldine is a teacher, our girls had a smooth introduction to academia, as their mother was their kindergarten teacher one day a week. I made it a point to bring the girls to their

Flying 'U' Ranch, 70 Mile House, 2010

first day of school, as I knew what a momentous day that was to me when I started primary school. Now that my daughters are young adults, I text them "tip of the day" words of wisdom, that hopefully offer useful advice in their daily lives. We financed the education for both girls at Bishop's University in a small town in the Eastern Townships part of Québec. The girls chose the university and the program. As I write the eldest has completed her degree and the youngest has two more years to go. Both girls elected to take one semester abroad with the eldest having gone to Malta, and Selena plans to an overseas experience as well. With a solid foundation in place it is now up to the girls to create their own lives.

Graduation Letter

Congratulations on your high school graduation! It is the first step of many more I look forward to watching. For your journey I created the acronym HEROISMS as a life organization system that I will share with you. The idea of

Brandon, Selena, Lori, Francesca, Bill, and Geraldine, The Boathouse, West Vancouver, 2009

HEROISMS is to be brave, to tackle life and live on your own terms. I trust that there will be insights here that will help you in your journey.

Health

- Do not clog your arteries. Too much of our food is unhealthy. Find out how to keep your arteries clear and the benefits will help you live a longer and better life.

- For nutrition, consider three categories of food: A. the best; B. the okay in moderation; and, C. the foods to avoid. Write down the list and post it in your kitchen.

- Exercise six days a week, and stretch.

- Drink more water than you think you need, every day.

- A multi-vitamin may be okay, but the results are not conclusive. With the lack of sun here six months a year Vitamin D looks like a good one. Learn from nutritionists and see what they say, but be prepared to get different answers.

Education

- Expect your education to have taught you how to think, solve problems, and open your mind; however, to gain a successful career or business you will need additional skills; hard-work, persistence, and interpersonal intelligence.

- Stay close to your university's alma mater as you can help each other as life progresses.

- Be careful of too much theory and not enough application, as life is not a spectator sport. Be creative with what you know is important.

Relations – Family and Friends

- Connect with your oldest relatives and make a meaningful effort to get to know them and learn their stories while they are still with us. Learning your family tree is a good starting point.

- You will only be in love at most a few times in your life, so embrace it when you are in it. Marriage is best to pursue sometime after university and by the time you wish to have children, a narrow time range. Be especially careful whom you have as a partner during these years.

- Relationships are as fragile as a crystal vase, and once broken they are hard to repair. It is wise to treat your closest ones generously, and hope it will be reciprocated.

- By the time you complete your education your best friends in life have mostly been made. After university, life gets busy, and new, meaningful friendships are few.

- Keep your sibling as a close friend and look out for each other.

- Aristotle wrote that friendships come in three forms: friends of convenience (up to 50), friends of pleasure (up to 15) and the highest level, friends of virtue (up to 5). Consider yourself fortunate if you have at least one in the virtue category.

Occupation

- Trust and integrity are your foundation. Keep it solid.

- Be best in the world at something, likely a specialized niche.

- Work hard to accomplish your goals. There is no way around this.

- Choose short-term pain and long-term gain over short-term gain and long-term pain.

- When negotiating, ensure you bring value to the table so you come at it with strength.

- Practice public speaking. Toastmasters are great, but also watch TED talks; and even better, give a TED talk.

- Know how to write well.

- Understand math and at least the fundamentals of accounting.

- Learn some languages, and at the very least learn to say 'hello' and 'thank you' in the most spoken ones.

- Plan out your future, but live today. Start with the end in mind and work backwards to figure out the process in detail to get to where you want to go.

- Do things that are out of your comfort zone; be bold and take smart calculated risks. This is how you grow.

- Be wary of being put into a box that does not define who you are. You need to know yourself to align your position with yourself.

- When you do good things do not expect compliments but very possibly criticisms. Do not let that stop you from what you want to accomplish. After all, Steve Jobs at one time was fired from Apple, the company he founded.

- Do not jump too quickly to counteract criticism, as it may be a blessing in disguise. Learn from it.

- If you encounter an obstacle, think like a laser beam and fire through it. If you cannot find a solution to a problem, it does not mean there is no answer; it just means that you may not have found a creative answer. Keep looking.

- When you win, it will only partly be due to you, and when you lose it will also be only partly due to you, so be humble and accept each result as part of the mosaic of life.

- When you have a conflict, you will have three choices: live with it, fix it or leave it. You do not want to live with long-term conflict, which then leaves you the other two choices: fix it or leave it.

- Read the "The Art of War" as a classic on understanding how to deal with the various forms of conflict and strategy in life.

- Win-win situations are the best, so give that an honest try in your negotiations. If it does not work then you will have to fight, and you fight to win.

- Understand the three components of an organization: visionary, managerial, and technical and read "E-Myth Revisited."

- Know the difference between line and staff jobs. Line jobs are better. Persistence is more important than most qualities to achieve success. A train sitting idly does not take you places. It is as hard to stop a train, as it is to start it. Keep moving.

- Divide projects you undertake into three parts – it works.

- Politics is the reality of organizations. With ambition you need to consider having the following; organizational skills, a strong work ethic, the diplomacy to not offend anyone, the ability to establish relationships with people who can help your goals, and the foresight of the potential consequences if you decide to be in the front and centre of controversial issues.

Interests

- Sports, the arts, or the outdoors. Whatever it is, pursue it with passion, and if you succeed in your efforts, you can celebrate it, and if not, there are no regrets for you gave it your best.

- Choose interests that are a good complement and contrast from your main occupation. If you work in an office, the outdoors is often a good bet. To balance academia, for summer jobs I looked for position so that were: outdoors, physical, and social.

Society

- Choose an organization to volunteer with or start your own to make a difference. Do not expect anything in return, but do not be surprised if there is. It is better to focus on one area to work on deeply than it is to be spread too thin. As in your career decide what is the grand vision of your efforts here.

Money

- Learn personal finance, and how investments work. We live in a society that rewards entrepreneurialism where most people are not entrepreneurs. Use the system to your advantage. The Saturday business section of national newspapers is a good start, as is reading "The Richest Man in Babylon," and "The Wealthy Barber."

- Financial Independence will make a positive difference in most aspects of your life. Live in the moment, plan for the future, and prepare for various life emergencies since what can go wrong often does.

Spirituality

- Find meaning in life and reach beyond the cacophony of overt materialism and constant technology. In my case my teachers in high school made a difference, as did reading "The Way of the Peaceful Warrior" in my 20s, and "The Power of Now" in my 30s.

Finally, there is a lot to accomplish and time is fleeting. Consider making 100 Life Visions for your life and track its progress in your journal. I hope there were elements of HEROISMS, and its collage of reflections that resonated with you, and remember to live a life of **Passion, Beauty, and Creativity**.

PS If you read one book a month you will only be able to complete 744 books before you turn 80, so start soon!

Bowen Island Community School, 2012

Family Relations

Making a difference

One item on my 100 Life Visions was to make a difference in my parents' lives while they were still with us. In 2004 to tackle publishing two of my father's books through a self-publishing organization. My father's passion and hobby were landscape design and gardening. In 1968 he purchased acreage near Stowe, Vermont and began his journey to work the land to create his vision. In the summers he would go when he could to live his life of solitude. He would be a kindred spirit to Thoreau and Emerson.

During winters he wrote five books on landscape design. With self-publishing having evolved to create books on demand, I was able to create his first book, "Escapism into Landscapism," and followed this with "Seven Garden Types." There are three more manuscripts on my bookshelves.

Family's log cabin, near Stowe, Vermont 1980

A few years later in 2007 I would tackle doing something for my mother that would make a material difference in her life. I set out to find the best seniors' residence I could find to transition her from her apartment. The Manoir Westmount in Westmount Park near downtown Montreal worked out very well. The location, being connected to a conservatory and the elegant Westmount Public Library while overlooking tennis courts where I used to work, was perfect. After a waiting period, and reluctance on her part, she moved in to the new residence and loved it. I followed up on this by deciding to organize her final art show. I asked an artist colleague of my mother's in Montreal for suggestions on the best way to put on an art show and the response was less than encouraging. The essence was not to bother, as it is very difficult to get a show. I took this as a challenge and contacted the Westmount

Art Council and mentioned my hope of celebrating my mother's life of art, and since she was 89, it would be a fitting end to her art career. The Arts Council accepted my application and coordinated the entire show. Some paintings were sold, which made my mother very happy. It was not the money that was important to her but the recognition of her talents. My mother passed away 10 years later, so it was timely to create this show while she was still mobile.

In 1948, fourteen years before I was born, my parents lived in Switzerland. At the time, Switzerland was considered a poor country, and the significant per capita wealth of the country developing later. The government of the time had forced placement of children into farms and institutions intended for parents who needed funds to be able to work and contribute to the economy.

During Christmas of 2017 I spoke to my brother Andy about his time in Switzerland, and he reiterated the traumatic experience he had had along with my older brother Denis. My sister Margit was at home with my mother as she was born in 1948 while my father studied English in preparation for their move to Canada. Although I knew about this story told by my brothers, I wondered if there were any articles on the Internet about other children who went through the system. I researched using Google, going through Swiss articles that highlighted this history, and right away I found many. After reading a few, I came across a notice from the Swiss government that 300 million Swiss francs had been set aside for children who had gone through the harsh treatment, and amazingly the deadline to apply of March 31, 2018 was only six weeks from the time I was reading it! This had occurred 70 years earlier and I had happened to do my research just before the deadline! I called up my brothers and told them this amazing discovery. Denis applied and I handled the application for Andy since he is a brilliant artist but has no interest in managing administrative things. After months of back and forth correspondence and requests for documents I received a call that Andy's application was accepted and that funds were to be deposited into his bank account. Denis received his compensation even earlier. The amount was diluted over the thousands of victims but it was helpful and appreciated by them nonetheless.

Sometimes in life there is justice, and it is worth paying attention to opportunities that may be in front of you but you may not see them.

Eulogy for my father

October 3, 2012

My father, Budapest, 1935

Friends and family,

I found out recently that since my father was 97, and my mother 94 they could be one of the oldest couples on the planet in seven years. I spoke to my father who was articulate to the end, and he said, "I have no wish to establish this record."

What are the ways of being that lead to his long life? I observed the following with my father:

100% concentrated chemical DEET – to activate your immune system

Major food groups from the supermarket deli counter.

When chipmunks or mice take up residence in the cottage, including where you prepare your food. You do not eradicate them but make them your friends and call them "Chippy." This reduced his life stress.

Values were Christian, honesty, hard work, and a balance of intellectual activity with more natural landscaping pursuits.

I grew up knowing my father to have had more than his share of trying times, notably escaping communism with a young family, and losing a child. But there were highlights: his upbringing; meeting my mother, and becoming a lawyer, a junior judge, a cavalry officer, Harvard law librarian, tennis player, as well as a voracious reader and writer. He said that the number of books in his library surpassed those accumulated by Charles Dickens. He humorously added his own letters to the more formal ones after his name, using LLG, learned landscape gardener.

He was passionate about landscaping. We made the mistake of having my father stand last in line to meet guests at our wedding reception. The line stopped in the sweltering heat, while he showed his landscaping plans that he had in his pocket to each of the guests and would invite anyone down who would like to come.

To me, going to the Vermont cottage was a base for friends from where to go and enjoy the nearby lake and village of Stowe. Now that we have our own place on a lake, I have a deeper understanding of what my father was looking for: a peaceful and necessary respite from the daily chess game of life. Maybe it is genetic as I too am now landscaping.

My father speaking at our wedding, Montreal, 1990

A poem my father read at our wedding:

Count your garden by the flowers. Never by the leaves that fall.

Count your days by golden hours. Don't remember clouds at all.

Count your nights by stars. Not shadows.

Count your years with smiles. Not tears.

Count your blessings. Not your troubles.

Count your age by friends. Not years.

At my father's celebration of life, Montreal, 2012

Eulogy for my mother

March 11, 2017

My mother and grandmother, Budapest, 1925

Friends and family,

Passion, Beauty, and Creativity. After long reflection, these are the words I came up with to encompass the essence of the life I aim to live. I could have saved myself the turmoil. All I would have had to do was to think of my mother's life as she embodied these three qualities, and I will share these with you today.

In organizing this celebration of life, I was fascinated with how many friends my mother still had at 99 years old! For those who are here, we are glad you could share this day with us.

Passion – For nature, especially birds and flowers. She loved drawing at the Montreal Botanical Gardens and was for years a member of the Japanese Pavilion there. She was not a fan of going to my parents' log cabin in Vermont; it was too rustic, and really my father's passion. If anyone saw the television show, Green Acres, with the lawyer husband wanting to get back to the land and his Hungarian wife wanting to stay in the big city – that was my parents. My mother said, "Why should I go and toil in the dirt when there are 300 gardeners at the Botanical Gardens making everything spectacular for us?" I continue to find interesting things in my mother's files as I recently discovered a letter from Maria von Trapp, from The Sound of Music fame, who owned a property close to ours in Stowe.

Beauty – For her art and of other artist's works. She sought excellence but not fame nor fortune in her art. Once a local television station asked if they could come and interview her, but she declined. She preferred to focus on her prolific works in relative solitude. Going through her letters I found one from Canadian Group of Seven artist Arthur Lismer, attesting to courses she had taken with him for over three years.

*My mother teaching Francesca
how to draw, Montreal, 1997*

Beauty for the life she had before the war with ballroom dancing, and the elegance of the prewar period in Budapest and travels in Europe. I found a photo of her as a teenager in Florence, and on the same trip she had gotten lost on the trails in Capri, and with her Latin she spoke to a priest who had brought her back to safety. In her courtship days my father had a competitor for my mother's affections. This fellow challenged my father to a sword fight to win the honour of my mother. My father said, "Yes, if you wish, but instead how about we just let Margit decide?" He already knew the answer. I heard this story many times growing up. She spoke five languages: Hungarian, German, Latin, English and French. My grandfather, a well-known architect, offered her a trip to join him on a research voyage to India when she was a teenager and she declined thinking she could do this later in life which then never materialized. She realized later that this was a mistake. I learned from that and I make an effort not to let good opportunities pass by.

The good times before the war were counterbalanced with her life's multiple tragedies and serious challenges that are now best left unsaid. After the upheavals of the war and her Budapest upbringing, she also lived in Geneva, Zurich, Ottawa, Boston, and Montreal.

Upon arriving in Canada my parents rented a home right across the street from the Governor General's Residence in Ottawa. Occasionally she had to go and find my brothers, who would be playing on the large property of the Governor General. Her children did take their turns adding to her life's stress. Coming over the Atlantic, my brother, Denis, could not be found on the boat and the frantic search finally ended by finding him safe and sound hiding on the deck. She loved my wife Geraldine, and her grandchildren.

Visiting the girls' grandmother, Westmount, 2007

Friends

Aristotle wrote that you could normally have a maximum of five best friends, 15 good friends, and up to 50 tertiary friendships. I came up with my own classification of friends:

Level I, Best friends

Best friends are trustworthy, have your best interests in mind, are open to discuss personal matters, and may be counted upon to help in whatever shape is needed when circumstances dictate. Mutually appreciated humour is another attribute.

You are fortunate if you have at least one Level I friend. It is likely that most Level I friends are made by the time you complete formal education. The depth of time spent with each other during school years along with many years of shared experiences are much less likely by the time you get established into a career and you start a family. There are only so many hours you can devote to friendships once the demands of family life are upon us.

Level II, Good friends

You enjoy each other's company, have good chemistry and both of you make an effort to make contact at least periodically. You can call this level of friend and ask or give a favour and be comfortable about giving or receiving. The key here is that each of you makes the effort, and if only one of you does then this friendship becomes a Level III friendship.

Level III, Tertiary friends

You both like each other, have good chemistry and enjoy each other's company even if there is little contact. Do not discount this level as it also offers mutually beneficial opportunities.

As you grow, friendships change and may move between the levels or in and out of the levels altogether. Beyond these levels constitutes acquaintances and you may have 1,000 or more of these depending on your profession and lifestyle. Most of my Level I and II friends come from a history that is either from academia or other learning-related activities, e.g. when I started two careers and the weeks of training needed to start those professions. A few close friendships are more valuable, allowing for a depth of experience that you will not have with the tertiary level of friendships.

> *Call your friends on their birthdays, as that is a sign that you have them in mind.*

I organize an annual tradition for my friends at our cottage. I invite a maximum of five friends, six including myself to an annual cottage "guys weekend," and I put great care into seeing what I can do to make this the best weekend of the year for my friends. I come up with a theme every year and look for new and creative ideas. Some of the things I have done in the past include having invited a mentalist for a show just for the six of us, a "Feast for Kings" catered by a French chef, and a cruise to Jedediah Island.

Annual guys weekend: From left; John, Bruce, Peter, Andrew, Ted, and Rod, Sunshine Coast, 2018

I find two levels of gatherings work best, either intimate ones with six or less or a large gathering allowing for multiple interactions between many guests. The reason I choose six as a maximum is because this group allows for everyone to sit comfortably together in a living room or outdoors around a fire pit; it is great for playing cards and a good fit for being on the dock. A group larger than this will start splitting into subgroups so the communal interaction is lost. With six, you may also generally use one vehicle to move around, and the level of organization is manageable. The composition of a group of a maximum of six may be one, two, or three couples, or for the "guys weekend" of all-male friends. Other things I like to do is to make notes of what specific things a guest would enjoy, e.g. for a wine connoisseur, I will find out what are his favourite reds and have some in the wine rack ready for him. If someone loves to hike, I will start the weekend after picking him up at the airport and climb the grueling "Grouse Grind," a very steep hike in North Vancouver, before heading up to the cottage. It is a creative exercise planned well in advance to ensure every detail is covered. An agenda is created to ensure logistics are smoothly taken care of. One thing I have learned over the years is that you can never have enough hors d'oeuvres. Whatever snacks are provided will be consumed in no time. Having multiple areas for food works well too. A tradition I began is to steam shrimp dumplings and while everyone is on the dock, I surprise them by coming down with a professional chef jacket and serving the hot dumplings out of a bamboo container, which is a hit. Of the core group of friends I invite, four of us have cottages and it was discussed that someone else would host one of the gatherings.

If you have strong friendships, it is wise to treat them very well and you hope it will be reciprocated.

Annually I arrange annually a meeting of another gathering of friends apart from cottage group. I organize it at the Wedgewood Hotel, the nicest ambiance I have found in Vancouver with live piano, large comfortable chairs, and elegant interior design. We meet in December, which is a good time to wind down before the holidays. I also enjoy one-on-one meetings with people at the same place. When in Whistler, the Mallard Lounge in the Château Whistler is another favourite meeting place with subdued live music, spacious and comfortable seating, and private areas.

Research the finest place in your city where it is the most conducive to have small group social gatherings as a great way to periodically meet with your friends.

CHAPTER SIX

OCCUPATION – YOUR MISSION

"Those who have found some sense of mission have a very special joy, which no one can take from them."

Richard Nelson Bolles

Starting Out

Lifeguard

I augmented my high school swimming by getting a Bronze Medallion in order that I could work as a lifeguard. The course was held at the Montreal Olympic stadium swimming pool. Since the 1976 Olympic games were only four years before, it was a fabulous facility to swim in. The diving pools could generate powerful bubbles for the divers to soften the entry into the water, and there was a deep diving pool for PADI certifications.

I sought out work as a lifeguard because I wanted a skilled summer job. I also liked the idea of being outdoors to contrast the endless indoor hours, especially in a climate like Montreal where it is cold for half of the year. I lifeguarded at the Westmount swimming pool in the late summer of 1981 after I returned from a job working with my friend Steffen out west. Later, I took the much higher-level National Lifeguard Service (NLS) course and I passed on my third attempt, a reminder to never give up. I completed the NLS no longer for work purposes but to finish something I did not complete previously.

Reflecting on my life direction, Old Fort Point, Jasper, 1987

"Nothing in the world can take the place of persistence. Talent will not, nothing is more common than unsuccessful men with talent. Genius will not, the world is full of educated derelicts. Persistence and determination alone are omnipotent."

Calvin Coolidge

White-Water Rafting Guide

As I felt that I pursued my education and my first job without a break, I decided I needed as such after two years of work, and then, I requested and was granted a leave in the summer of 1987. This was also due to thinking I was in a job I wanted to grow out of and I would need time to make decisions on my future career. I again drove out west, this time with my friend Bruce, and we spent a wonderful summer in Jasper where I worked as a white-water rafting guide for two teachers who owned the company. It was very well run and the owners Bryn and Ron, were excellent proprietors and generous with the guides. Guiding did not offer a pension plan or stock options; however, it I did give me the chance to be outside in the beautiful wilderness and meet interesting people.

Shooting rapids, Athabasca River, Jasper, 1987

I lived in a camper van, while I spent days shooting the rapids with guests from the Jasper Park Lodge and evenings with Bruce, or Marion an attractive lively woman I met at the Alberta Government Tourist office who introduced me to the owners of the rafting company I would work for.

My first vehicle, a 1983 Dodge Ram camper van

It was in Jasper where I cleared my head and started to put more thought into what I wanted to pursue in life. I did not have all the answers but at least I had the creative downtime to reflect. I came up with some thoughts. Initially I would go back to Toronto to my position at Canadian Pacific before I made my next move.

Career

Computers

I graduated in 1985 after a recession and landed an interview with Canadian Pacific (CP) for their Computers and Communications division in Toronto. I was up against another graduate who had the highest marks coming out of the same university program I was in. Being comfortable socially helped me win the job. At first, programming required me to write code in a cubicle and I embraced the job but it was not an ideal fit for my more outgoing personality.

On the first day of training at CP, I met Andrew, a native Torontonian who became a good friend while I was in the city. Many years later in 2006 we reconnected since we were both living on the West Coast, he in Seattle and I in Vancouver. On the day of the 1987 stock market crash Andrew and I walked over to the Toronto Stock Exchange and watched the action from the viewing stands. Since history shows that periodic crashes occur and without exception there is a recovery to new highs, I recognized it would soon be an excellent entry point to invest. Although at the time I worked in technology, I still held a strong interest in the investment profession as it offered a career with real potential, the ability to work for clients to help achieve their goals, and it would facilitate buying a home, as well as a cottage which I would eventually build. I did not have material interests much beyond this, as I was mostly interested in living a meaningful life.

On occasion, Andrew and I would go up to his cottage in Muskoka, which was great since my family's cottage in Vermont was a long trek from Toronto for a weekend. One perk of my job included the benefit of parking on CP Rail land close to where I lived at Harbourfront. Eventually the Toronto Skydome would be built where I used to park my van by a railroad track. Living downtown I could walk to work, which was convenient, but I missed nature, and I resolved this through future living arrangements on the West Coast.

My position changed internally, where I then had to install train monitoring computer systems across Canada. This was a much more interesting position, due to the travel, and I enjoyed visiting different railway towns, and meeting people. Nelson, BC was a notably great trip where I combined the required work with a day off skiing in Whitewater. Since I was living in a concrete urban landscape, the beauty of small-town Nelson impressed me. At the time in 1987 a small house could be purchased for $30,000. This was a year before a well-known film, *Roxanne*, was filmed in the picturesque small town. Years later I would move to BC with Geraldine and settle on the coast and buy homes at far higher prices.

After leaving CP and volunteering at the Calgary Olympics I moved back to Montreal and looked for my next career move. I took on an office automation position at General Electric, while working as a white-water rafting guide on the weekends where I would shoot rapids on the Rivière Rouge near Montebello, Québec. The rafting was a healthy balance to the computer work during the week, although working seven days a week did not leave room for much else. I enjoyed the job at GE but I wanted to go back to university to explore computers and architecture. After one year I resigned at GE and went to the University of Colorado, Denver for graduate studies.

Computers and Architecture

Making the decision to go to graduate school was not an easy one considering Geraldine and the expense of university in the US was barely feasible. I completed one semester and enjoyed the experience but instead decided to go back to Montreal and see if I could continue my vision in Canada where it would be more financially feasible and I could also be with Geraldine. This decision worked out in the end, but it would take me a few years to get my career back on track. I found Computer Assisted Design (CAD) work for an architect in Montreal who had a contract work with Air Canada. The people I met at Air Canada offered me to take on a consulting role at the Dorval International Airport now called Pierre Elliott Trudeau Airport where I created CAD drawings for the facilities management department. It was a good work environment and I stayed in touch with some of the coworkers for years. It was at Air Canada that I started working out during my lunch hour since they had an onsite gym facility. I never looked back and 30 years later working out at lunch is still part of my routine.

Geraldine in the meantime decided to pursue a teaching degree and she was accepted at UBC in Vancouver. Since I was on contract, I supported the idea and we moved to Vancouver where I would pursue my next career move. My real raison d'être in life was to be involved in something interesting and refuse to live a life of mediocrity. Now that I had CAD skills, I pursued this, and though I combined both work in this field with more architecture courses, it did not lead me in the direction I wanted to go. I then took on a business development role also in the CAD world, that taught me professional client acquisition skills, which allowed us to slowly plan out a brighter future. While working full time I decided that taking advantage of my business degree was the wisest thing I could do, and then I looked at getting into what I thought I would do in university, namely go into the investment field. While working full time I studied in the evening and completed the Canadian Securities Course as my first of many steps into this career.

Wealth Management

This time before choosing a career, I spent one year learning exactly what I was getting myself into, and I counted that I had up to 20 interviews or meetings with people in the industry. I did not take the first offer that came to me and took the time to learn as much as possible. I decided that choosing a company that had a strong training program would be the right place to begin. I learned that a new West Vancouver office of ScotiaMcLeod would be opening soon, which would open opportunities for new advisors.

Although the timing was not perfect, which it almost never is, I made the move. During the multiple interviews I once had to leave our house early, and, not wanting to wake up Geraldine and Francesca, I dressed in the dark and left quietly. On my ferry commute I noticed that I had put on an unmatched pair of dress shoes! Fortunately, they were both black. There was no time to return home or buy new shoes before the interview at a trust company. In a situation like this the best thing to do is to adapt and deal with it. I decided that after I met the interviewer, I would quickly sit down at a desk where the shoes would not be an issue. I arrived early but the reception was not open yet so I waited in the elevator area. A woman came out of an office door and looked at me and slowly moved her eyes down and locked onto my shoes as if she were psychic! I put one leg behind the other so it was not so obvious I had the mismatched shoes. She then left and the interviewer came out to greet me. We had a good discussion and he never noticed the shoes. There was no immediate job with that firm, and I went on to have other interviews in the industry before I accepted a trainee role as a Financial Advisor with ScotiaMcLeod.

Phase I

The directive for new rookie advisors in 1997 was to go out and get $20 million in assets under management as quickly as possible to keep your job. Starting from scratch without already having a client base is a challenging exercise. In my training program there were 21 rookies, and when I left the firm 15 years later, there were four of us left, which is considered normal. There was not much balance in the first five years, as I had to quickly decide which on what type of wealth management system I was going to use and how I was going to attract clients. More than any other quality, persistence was the component that allowed me to eventually thrive. In the beginning I made an effort to meet both lawyers and accountants, which produced some results. The high-tech industry in which I used to work had given me contacts to connect with potential investors, and I made modest gains here. My first real success was making the decision to reach out to my alma mater. My reasoning was that the further you reside from where you studied, the warmer a call from a fellow graduate would likely be - one that and could result in gaining new clients. Since I lived in Vancouver and my studies took place in Montreal, this worked well. However, if you worked in Montreal and were calling graduates from McGill, it could still work but may not be as effective considering it is not unique. The best yet is, if you studied somewhere far away like Paris and you then connected with graduates living in Vancouver - now *that* would be excellent. By the end of the first year I met the firm's required $5 million target. The next year the target was now $10 million, which I had achieved as well.

In my third year the requirement was to get to reach $15 million, which I also accomplished, helped by a referral to a new client with a very large portfolio, which then qualified me for Executive Council, a weekend conference that was meant to show newer advisors on track to what was possible and take us to the next level. The year 2000 was also the year of the high-tech bubble burst. Fortunately, I took profits on most of my technology positions, which significantly cushioned the downturn.

In 2001 the world changed with the terrorist attack on the World Trade Centre in New York. Living on the West Coast I was on a 5:30 a.m. ferry on the way to work when a fellow commuter who was in his car, heard the news of the first plane crash and came up to tell others about it. At the time it immediately sounded like it may have been a terrorist attack and there was little doubt after getting to work and seeing the second plane crash.

A friend from university married a woman living in New York who was working for a bond trading company on the upper floors of the World Trade Centre. She left her job sometime before the 9/11 tragedy and moved to the U.K. to be with her new husband. The marriage ended quickly and she moved back to New York but she could not get her job back at the World Trade Centre. With her marriage dissolved she may have considered this unfortunate, but was it? It likely saved her life.

Life is a series of experiences and successes may be failures and failures may be successes. We can rightly be humble in knowing this.

The unimaginable human tragedy and world-changing consequences aside, the world regrouped and continued on, and after a brief sharp shock to the markets they recovered and went on to new highs. This is another reminder that attaching market forecasts to geopolitical events is difficult at best and applying asset allocation and systems in portfolios that take into consideration various outcomes is the prudent way to deal with the multitude of unknowns including black swan events.

During my first three years, I made a good decision by focusing on six investment strategies, which eventually evolved into Six Investment Models™. Why six? Because one was too few and ten was too many. By focusing, I could offer well-reasoned models that clients could mix and match. In 2007 I ran for and won the role of finance director of the Canadian Paralympic Committee, and this, along with the Vancouver Olympic and Paralympic Games coming in 2010, as well as my health and my health issue in 2009, diverted a lot of time from researching new protocols, and I kept the status quo of the models that were working.

To top this off in 2008 there was a financial crisis and a third stock market crash I witnessed. The crash was set off by the sub-prime lending in the US that brought Wall Street to its knees and the risk that the financial system would shut down was not

Opening the Toronto Stock Exchange with Paralympic curler, Chris Daw and Canadian Paralympic Foundation, 2007

only real but it was diverted with only hours to go. Yet again this was another time to add to your portfolio for those who had the stomach to step up to the plate when the news was doom and gloom. As an advisor I needed to point out to clients that history has shown that the market has always recovered from these shocks, so the best strategy was to stick with the systems that were predetermined to deal with shocks. What if the financial system really did shut down? Then there would be no immediate liquidity, like owning private equity or real estate. Eventually liquidity would have to be sorted out and the system would be restarted.

Phase II

In 2018 I finally grew the practice to over $50M with over 100 families, a long overdue objective achieved.

I was content with my Six Investment Model™ although I did not have an aggressive investing option. I focused on low-to-moderate-risk investing because I did not want clients to lose money but also because I never found a more aggressive rules-based, time-tested model that was compelling enough to offer clients, at least not until later.

Wall Street, New York, 2008

When I retrieved my notes on momentum strategies, I realized that this was worthy of exploring further. After reading multiple books on momentum I decided that this was a perfect addition to my Six Investment Models™. I found a way to introduce Momentum Rotation while maintaining the integrity of my existing systems.

In 2019, I officially started testing and tracking Momentum Rotation in my own account and I was very satisfied with the results. So far so good. I then launched Model 5: Momentum Rotation for clients who wanted a more aggressive option. My expectation was that this model should double the market rate of return, e.g. if the market returned 7.5%, I would reasonably expect 15.0% in momentum. Since my Model 4: Growing Dividends had returned 10.0% over 17 years ending in 2019, in order to justify the momentum strategy I would need significantly more than the 10.0% to make the offering worthwhile.

With Kevin O'Leary of the "Shark Tank" & "Dragon's Den," Vancouver, 2012

Phase III

I am currently working on bringing my practice up to managing $100 million for the balance of my career. The benefit of having achieved Phase II is that I can focus on client portfolios and there is no pressure to have to grow the practice unless I want to. Since I am ambitious, I will give Phase III a spirited effort. You can argue to set your financial goals higher, however I enjoy optimizing all parts of HEROISMS and not just the "M" part. In order to get to Phase III I am using a combination of 1. Offering both an outstanding mix of Six Investment Models™, and, 2. A systemized client servicing process for referrals; and 3. Keeping a database of advisors who are retiring within a few years. While working on Phase III I will look to build my team for expanded overage for clients.

A break from partners' meetings with a helicopter tour of the Grand Canyon, 2018

Wisdom from a Hermit

In 2000, I asked the head of our training department if there was an advisor in the company who took a systemized rule-based approach to investing and employed some outstanding and scalable methods. She replied, "Yes, Robert has done very unique things." I said, "Great, may I get an introduction?" She replied, "I do not advise this, since Robert is a different cat and sticks to himself." I ended up meeting him at a conference in Banff, Alberta, seven years later in 2007 where he gave a talk on his investment philosophy. I was mesmerized by what I was looking for all along. Robert gave out copies of his book, "Investing on Autopilot, Strategies that really work and how you can profit from them," and I then studied it in the evenings of the conference. Robert spoke more than once so different advisors could attend his lecture. I returned to the same lecture twice. This was a turning point of how I currently manage my practice.

By now I was managing over $40 million and working on getting to Phase II of $50 million, which is considered a solid long-term practice to manage. Coincidentally, Robert had six models as well and had a scientific mind that scrutinized ways to beat the market. In my earlier education there were presentations within the investment industry on how one *cannot* beat the market so instead advisors should focus on asset allocation and top-notch client servicing and build a practice this way. As I later discovered there are repeatable ways to beat the market using approaches with a long track record. I made some enhancements to my models when I returned from the conference, and it took another decade before I fine-tuned my Six Investment Models™ to a level I thought optimal. I narrowed down two of the models that resonated with me and I highlighted a third, called 'momentum,' which I left for later review. I also learned that fine-tuning is a never-ending exercise, and when you think you have it just right, there will be some adjustment that continues this optimization process.

2007 was also the year I won an election to serve as Director of Finance for the Paralympic Committee, and this, combined with the 2010 Olympic and Paralympic Games coming to Vancouver, meant that I would put in a significant amount of effort on the volunteer front, which limited introducing new investment research initiatives until I was able to study, test, and implement them. To top it off in 2009 I had three stents put into my arteries, which meant another constraint on my time as I dealt with this issue.

In 2018 I learned that Robert was no longer with the firm where we both had worked, and I reached out to him when I saw that he had written a new book called "Inevitable Wealth - Two low-risk strategies that combine to create extraordinary wealth." I ordered the book, and it was clear Robert must have remembered me as he sent me the book with a personal note. We started an email dialogue that was Socratic in method and we have kept it up ever since. The feeling was one of asking questions to a Delphi oracle where I would have to patiently wait for a response. Since Robert lives a life of solitude, all communication to him goes through email and he likes it that way. Robert became a mentor who helped lead me to the most recent fine-tuning of my Six Investment Models™. He was educated as a scientist and engineer, hence his disciplined approach that I resonate with. I also pursued sciences as a diploma before my university degree in commerce. Unique to him is his focus on his research and leaving the client servicing to his team. He was proud to say that when he went into his office nobody recognized him. We differ in that I am 75% social while Robert is only 25%, not surprising for a private person. Robert would understand the likes of Emerson and Thoreau and he would appreciate that "the solution to loneliness is solitude," a phrase my father would echo at his Vermont log cabin.

In 2018 I dusted off "Investing on Autopilot," and realized that using momentum was a strategy that would be an outstanding element to fit into my models. Momentum investing is a rules-based approach to buying stocks that demonstrates the highest returns over a period of anywhere from three to twelve months. A rotation takes place of the stocks where the strongest companies are kept and the weakest removed. For further research I read other momentum gurus; James O'Shaughnessy's, "What Works on Wall Street," and Gary Antonacci's "Dual Momentum." After comparing alternatives, I adopted a strategy that Robert wrote about in his first book. Eleven years after I first learned about momentum, I went to the library and researched articles and tested with success a Momentum Rotation strategy in my own portfolio before I offered it to clients the following year.

My mentor is now retiring after ending a successful wealth management career built on a scientific approach to managing assets, respectfully recognized for the thorough analysis of his models. I will carry on many of his principles while adding some of my own.

CHAPTER SEVEN

INTERESTS – THE SPICE OF LIFE

"A man who wants to do something will find a way; a man who doesn't will find an excuse."

Stephen Dolley, Jr.

Sports

Hockey

Growing up in Montreal there was an outdoor hockey rink in most neighbourhood parks. In the 1970s there was a large volume of snow in the city and the rinks would have to be routinely shoveled, clearing away the huge piles. I enjoyed skating and playing hockey with my friends in what was a free-for-all without the safety focus you have today. Helmets were mostly absent these rinks. One day as I skated around the back of the net, another hockey player took a slap shot and the puck sailed over the net and grazed the pompom of my hat. Without a helmet on, was a close call. The bitter cold was not an issue as I eagerly headed off with my gear whenever I could. My high school also had an indoor hockey rink to use, and I was able to use the freshly cleaned ice early before school started without cost, and that was fabulous!

Like many kids growing up in Québec, ice hockey was complemented by watching the NHL, and playing street hockey. Years later in Vancouver I was invited to a function where the Stanley Cup was put on display. The guests took turns getting photos and kissing the cup. The things we did before COVID-19. I picked up the large cup to see how heavy it was, and it was very manageable. I called up a friend from Edmonton who happened to be in Vancouver and knowing he was a hockey fan I said he should come over and see the cup, expecting this to be a big deal for him. He said, "Thank you, but I have already have had it on my kitchen table." The trophy clearly gets around.

The Stanley Cup weighs only 34.5 pounds, Vancouver, 2013

My hockey days ended in high school and I moved on to other sports; although, I enjoy watching the Winter Olympic hockey games every four years. I also keep a tabletop rod hockey game at our cottage for guests, especially for my friend, Steve, who I used to play it with me when we were teenagers. Being part of a life-size rod hockey game was fitting for my role in the closing ceremonies of the 2010 Winter Olympics.

Running

Being a goal setter, I decided days before the end of 1982 that in September of the following year I would run the Montreal marathon, nine months away. Although I loved sports in high school, running was not part of my routine. When I set out on a bitter cold day for my first run, I used a basic pair of Nike court shoes and I was only able to run a few blocks before having to take a break. This quickly progressed to many blocks, and then a kilometer. Soon I was running 2.5 km uphill to the scenic Westmount lookout point where I would stop and stretch. Not long after, I was able to run the 5 km return trip, and I then bought my first quality pair of running shoes. After numerous repetitive loops of this 5 km run, I had a breakthrough and I was able to keep going seemingly forever, running 15 km, then 20 km, even longer.

Break down goals into clearly articulated sub goals.

In the summer of 1983, I went to Austria and Hungary where I continued to run. Jogging around the city of Budapest was unusual at the time as I did not see anyone else do it until I went to Margit Island, where I saw a couple of runners. Running across the city's bridges at that time, one would likely be engulfed by diesel fumes from cars and trucks, but I would run through it, occasionally having to stop due to the smoke. I returned to Montreal in time to run a 35 km test run, and then shortly after completed my one and only marathon. After this race I continued to run but changed the distance to what I enjoy most, a 5.5 km trail run that I continue to this day. When I lived in Montreal, my normal running route would lead up to the Westmount lookout point and back. It was a steep climb towards the end with a view towards the city among fabulous mansions, many built in the early 1900s. To the left of the lookout there is a large stone mansion that was cut in half and converted into two separate large homes.

I prefer trail running, and one day I finally had my ideal course come to life when we moved to Vancouver and eventually Bowen Island. In the 26 years and 9 months of living on the island, there is an idyllic 5.5 km run in a forest that surrounds Killarney Lake. On average I have run this course at least once a week every year we have lived here, which works out to 7,612 kilometers. Since the distance from coast to coast in Canada is 6,521 kilometers, I have run more than the equivalent of running across the country just on these trails. Since the distance back and forth across the United States at the shortest distance works out to 7,514 kilometers (4,696 miles), I have also completed this equivalent return trip as well. On hot summer days I sometimes turn the run into my island version of a biathlon and stop at a picnic ground and dive off a rock into a lake for a refresher; I then put my running shoes back on and run the rest of the trail back to the starting gate across from the St. Gerard's Mission. I also installed a chin-up bar in my carport so I may enjoy an upper body workout along with my run. Over the years, there has been a bear on the trail, owls, as well as a toad infestation with so many, I had to watch every step to not harm any; surprisingly I never saw any deer even though the island is full of them. The deer clearly have their preferred stomping grounds, and I theorize that they prefer to be closer to human habitation since there is less risk of wild predators. I have tracked my time over the decades, and on one particular run I had my best time ever of 30:45. I jumped in celebration, amazed that I was 40 and still getting faster! That run was my fastest ever and I have not surpassed that time since. The fastest time came after spending time in Calgary at high altitudes, and upon returning I set out on the trails. The oxygenated blood gave me that extra boost but it only lasted one day before more normal times returned. Interestingly, running acts like a canary in a coalmine. In 2009 my sudden slower times on my trail run proved a wake-up call that something was wrong, which eventually alerted me to get stents put in before anything more serious like a heart attack could develop.

The chances of dying from a first heart attack may be as high as 50%. Have a leading indicator to warn you of closing arteries, like running.

Martial Arts

On top of beginning my career in Toronto in 1985, I also seriously took up martial arts. I began learning Karate in university, but it was at the Toronto Academy where I really focused on this sport and way of life. The combination of flexibility, focus, discipline, and self-defense made a real difference in my life, more than any other sport. In 1987 I went to Japan to travel the country and train at martial arts schools. The University of Tokyo had the most beautiful dojo I had ever seen. Another club I trained in had a warm-up session of punching a bag of wooden blocks, clearly a tougher place to work out. I trained at some clubs that let me in, though there were others that did only allowed training for members.

Martial arts training, Japan, 1987

The first serious hint that I may have a health issue occurred while I was at the Toronto Academy karate club. One day a group went for a run in the country where the instructor owned a place. What struck me odd was that during on this run I felt I was giving everything I had, yet I still found it difficult to keep up with the fastest runners. I noticed that I seemed to be working harder than the others who were running at the same speed. Why was this? I put it to genetics and not being a naturally fast runner but many years later I understood that this was due to clogged arteries. The fast action martial arts movements were not impacted by the restrictions in the arteries, but running at full speed did have a limiting effect. It would be 22 years later when I would get stents put in.

At the Toronto Academy I sparred with a fellow karate student and as I blocked his kick with my arm while, my fist hooked on the inside of my opponent's uniform. As he pulled back his kick, my fist became trapped and his pants ripped open from his feet to his waist. Everyone had a good laugh. The club I belonged to was unique in that there were philosophy lectures along with the physical practices. After three years of focused practice I received an advanced brown belt that I replicated in Montreal at the Shidokan club when I moved back there. In Toronto the club deemphasized competition and focused on inner growth, while with the Montreal club I participated at an international competition at the University of Connecticut and won 1st place in one competition and 3rd in another.

Martial arts made a big difference in my life, Montreal, 1990

When we moved out west, I picked up other sports. The six focused years of karate still come back to benefit me in various ways. Quick reaction time and knowing how to fall without injury are some of the benefits.

"Research your own experience. Absorb what is useful. Reject what is useless. Add what is specifically your own."

Bruce Lee

Swimming

I love fresh water, whether it is lakes or rivers. Oceans are majestic in their own right but to me do not offer the tranquility, warmth and cleanliness of fresh water. Growing up in Montreal West, I joined a swim team in high school that was rigorous in its standards. Training started early in the morning consisting of endless laps. Donna was the head coach of the swim team, and she was well respected in Canadian swimming. She drove an early version of a Honda car where the letters on the back were rearranged and an extra 'N' added to spell "DONNA." Once while training, I recall the endless laps to be getting monotonous so I switched from crawl to the sidestroke. Donna yelled out "that is not a competitive stroke!" Races were held in pools across Montreal's West Island. I also joined my high school swim team, which proved the perfect antidote for my hyperactive self. The few years of swimming did set a foundation for related activities, including working as a lifeguard and white-water rafting guide, and also two open water long-distance swims. One cold open ocean swim spanned was from Boyer Island to Bowen Island near West Vancouver, which took an hour and half to complete, and my hands were so numb after the swim that I had to thaw in a hot tub for half an hour.

I researched activities that were physically challenging but which nobody has recorded. I considered where my strengths lay and swimming proved a good choice. After looking at various locations for a long-distance swim, I chose Sakinaw Lake on the Sunshine Coast since this lake has warm fresh water, and has a reasonable distance of seven kilometers. I contacted officials on a committee overseeing the lake and they said there was not any officially recorded swim of the length of the lake. I selected August 29, 2001, as the date to tackle this exercise, and I arranged an acquaintance and two of her friends to ride along in a safety boat and track me in the estimated three-and-half-hour swim. The lake is oddly shaped and therefore, it is open to interpretation what constitutes a swim of the length of the lake. I decided that swimming from Sakinaw Lake Road on the north end of the lake to Lee Road near the south end was essentially the length of the lake, and logistically, it worked well. After smearing on some Vaseline and climbing into a wet suit I plunged into the lake from the communal landing dock and started to swim. I chose swimming from North to South based on advice since this was the direction of the current, which ended up being a mistake. The head wind from the ocean funnels up the lake like a bat out of hell and proves much more powerful than any current going in the opposite direction. I swam crawl for a long time but switched to breaststroke as I found it better to navigate my direction and judge the waves. About half way into the swim the three women in the safety boat who were tracking my swim had to leave to briefly go to shore and I was left in the middle of the lake without a life buoy. I now know what a shipwrecked sailor feels like for the 15 minutes I was out there on my own. A motorboat went by, not too far away from me, and I could see the occupants wondering what I was doing in the middle of the lake. I waved them on. As the wind picked up, fighting the current became harder and it required effort to avoid being dragged backwards. Erin who was on the safety boat had a water access cottage near the other end of the lake and across the road where my planned finish line awaited. As the road came within viewing distance, I spoke to her about changing the final destination from the road to looping around some islands and ending at her place. She said this change in the course was similar in distance to going to the road. I elected to go to her cottage as the ending point as psychologically the distance seemed better as I was very tired after swimming for over five hours. I arrived at the cottage five and a half hours later. If I would have swum in the other direction, I may have completed my swim in less than four hours.

After a few hugs we crossed over to the bottom of Lee road; I said my goodbyes and drove back to the ferry and to West

Swimming the length of 7km Sakinaw Lake, 2001

Vancouver. It was too late to get back home to Bowen Island, and instead I stayed at the Park Royal Inn for the night, which has since been since then demolished. My knees felt inflamed from the endless breaststroke that put a lot of stress on my joints. I soaked in a bathtub to recover and for a couple of days I could not walk without some difficulty. On September 2, 2001, the <u>Coast Reporter</u> published an article of my swim, and The World Openwater Swimming Ass. also kept a record.

It was news at the moment, but not if I had swum a few days later, as the world changed on September 11, 2001, and my modest personal achievement would have been overshadowed by the world changing tragedy of 9/11.

Skiing

Skiing down a mountain holding torches on New Year's Eve was part of my 100 Life Visions. We were vacationing in Whistler during the Christmas week holiday of 2009 when at 5:00 p.m. on New Year's Eve, I read in the <u>Pique</u> Whistler newspaper that everyone was invited to come out and watch the torch parade come down the mountain to bring in the New Year. I could not believe my eyes: this was on my 100 Life Visions and it was happening in 60 minutes! I did not want to watch; I wanted to ski! I called

Whistler Mountain and asked who organizes the event. Customer relations did not know who this was and replied, "It is run by a different group and not the mountain." I asked, "Okay who might know who I should speak to?" Again, they had no idea. I then thought who do I know in Whistler, and I remembered having lunch with a group in Torino, Italy during the 2006 Paralympics and Ken Melamed, the Mayor of Whistler being part of the group. I looked up his name in the phone book, and lo and behold, he answered the phone on New Year's Eve. I said, "Hello Ken, this is Peter Boronkay. Thank you for taking this call on New Year's Eve. We met in Torino, and I am in Whistler and wonder if you know who organizes the torch relay, as I would love to do this." He replied, "Sure, speak to Brian of Ski Patrol." He gave me his number and I called Brian. He also answered the phone and I explained that though I knew it was last minute, I would appreciate joining the group for the torch relay. He said, "You are far too late as we are full and we also have a waiting list." I said, "I understand. If I show up and a spot becomes available, may I join in?" He said, "You can do as you like, but I cannot guarantee a spot if you show up."

I changed into my ski gear and drove to the Whistler parking lot. I hauled my skis over to the Whistler gondola. Outside there were more than 100 people who were scheduled to go up that evening. I joined a group of older skiers, and I explained my predicament. Someone said, "Do not worry, just stick with us and we will get you up." Yes, there is hope! As 6:00PM approached everyone lined up to the gondola. A staff person was checking names before the skiers were getting on the lift. When it was my turn one of the fellows instructed the young lady to write down my name on her list, as I was a last-minute guest in the group I joined. She did, and next thing I knew I was loading into the gondola and heading up! We arrived at the Roundhouse Lodge and a surreal experience unfolded. Having been there countless times during the day, it was now a pitch-dark, snowy and windswept landscape. The only light came from two bonfires that were lit on either side of the line of skiers. As the skiers approached the bonfires, we were given two torches, which we had to dip into the fires, and when lit, we would follow the person in front of us without poles and snake our way down intermediate runs of the mountain. It took half an hour to ski the trails from the Roundhouse all the way into the village. As we approached the village, the crowds were out clapping and noise making as they do in ski races, and I was greeted at the bottom by well-wishers, including Geraldine and the girls. It was a most memorable moment.

"Half of success in life is showing up."

Anonymous

Curling

After attending the Olympic Academy of Canada in Calgary in 2004, I made one of my goals to give it a serious attempt at competing internationally in a sport. Being 42 I had to limit my options, and thus, narrowed down my choices to curling. I went ahead and assembled a curling team with the following inspiration: Because Canada is a curling power and I had read that Hungary was building their first curling rink, I would put together a team of Canadians with Hungarian heritage that could potentially be the best Canadian-Hungarian curling team in the world. I had to do research on who would qualify to be on the team based on dual nationality and who either already knew how to curl or who would be willing to train to get to a high skill level. I researched, interviewed, and took on a high-performance coach, Brad, who was also was doing work with the Korean national curling team. We worked together for one and a half years before an international tournament in Europe in 2005. I pulled together a team of curlers, one of whom was a high-performance curler who became Skip, while the rest of the team members included already competent curlers and two new curlers including myself, who made up the team. The CBC picked up on the story and interviewed me on two occasions. The training and the logistics were both a significant drain on my time while I was building a wealth management practice. It was difficult but we kept at it, training after work whenever possible at multiple clubs around the Vancouver area. Our team attended a high-performance curling camp in Mills Bay on Vancouver Island in the summer of 2005. It was unusual to be curling indoors on ice in the summer but it was necessary to get up to speed leading up to the year-end competition. The Canadian national woman's curling team was also training at this camp.

As December rolled around, our team was without a coach, as he had other international commitments when our team headed to Budapest. We played a number of rounds winning all games except for one tie and one loss, until we made the finals. In the final game our competition was led by the financier of the new curling club and the Skip of the Hungarian national curling team. We won the match to end with a gold! I presented the club with a Canadian flag signed by Olympian and World Champion curlers as a gift to the new curling club. The flag is hanging in the club as a memory of their country's first international curling competition and our

Canadian team's contribution to it. On the long flight home, I reflected on whether this project could go to another level and see our team compete at these championships. After much thought, I decided that the logistics made this unlikely and winning this international tournament was an excellent end to our project. Tyler, the Skip, said the tournament gold was the highlight of his curling career. The curling project played on my strengths of being organized and having the ability to gather interest for a project, and putting in the pieces to make the vision come to reality. The price to pay was the time commitment while juggling a career and two young children. I could not have done this without Geraldine's support.

Canadians win first international tournament in Hungary

"[Dec 15, 2005] The Boronkay Team based out of Vancouver won gold ... at the first international curling competition held in Hungary (Budapest) December 2-4, 2005. The team beat out 15 other curling teams from Europe including such established curling nations such as Switzerland, and Austria. The final match was won on the last rock by one point to finish the game ... 7-6."[1]

From left: Wayne, Tyler, Mat, Peter and Steve

Golf

While growing up in Montreal West, the Meadowbrook Golf Club, previously known as Wentworth, featured it's "hole 3" across some railroad tracks near where I lived, and I would head over there with friends during the summer to walk around the course and during the winter to cross country ski on the grounds. Even in early high school I thought golf would be an enjoyable sport to pick up; although, I perceived it as an expensive activity that was beyond my parents finances and my paper route budget to get involved in. I now know that there are programs available that encourage youth to get involved in golf at many clubs, which would make it affordable for them to start the sport.

Putting at age twelve (on left)

After university, I did play occasionally up until 2005, when a new 9-hole golf course was built on Bowen Island. Since I had completed my curling project, I thought it was a good time to actively pick up the sport as something I can carry forward in life. The board of directors for the newly built course offered a unique lifetime charter membership opportunity. If you were to buy a charter membership, you would get the following: "unlimited play for life with no green or any other annual fee, for your lifetime, the opportunity to pass your membership on to one of your children for their lifetime, also with unlimited play, or if you moved away and sold your house, you could attach your membership to your house for the new buyer." In theory, the latter could translate to a recovery of up to the $18,000 of the purchase price. I number-crunched the opportunity and if you were a regular player this was reasonable, and it was also a chance to help a new golf club in its start-up stage. I went ahead with the charter membership and enjoyed this beautiful course with the final hole overlooking the ocean. Within a year after joining the club changed its policy and annual fees were introduced for charter members, which they said was needed to keep the club going. Although this negated most of the financial benefit of the charter purchase, it remains a great course and a credit to the founder who thought big and executed on his vision.

In 2010 we bought a lakefront property that our family would use on the weekends, and I would go back to playing golf occasionally. Now that the cottage project is complete I could revisit more time with this great sport. After volunteering for the 2010

Bowen Island Golf Club, 2009

Olympics and Paralympic games I looked for ways to contribute to golf, and I contacted Golf Canada where they offered me a role on their Investment Committee, that I have contributed to for over nine years.

Motorcycling

In 2016 I started thinking about what could I could learn and do that I have not yet done before. I thought about how I had never had a motorcycle. I knew that the time commitment to regular would not fit into my schedule and Geraldine had no interest either. I decided to set the objective of learning how to ride and get comfortable with it this over a summer and that would be sufficient for my objective. This way if I ever wanted to pick up riding again, I could do so with experience behind me. I signed up for a course in North Vancouver in March of 2017. The weather can be awful at that time of year, but I was fortunate as it was clear and sunny. I decided on a bike that would best suit my summer of riding - a

Yamaha XT250, the same one Sylvester Stallone used in one of his films. I chose the bike not because of the film association, but because it was a dual-purpose on-road off-road bike that I could use to explore the back roads of the Sunshine Coast. The course went well and I picked up my new bike with all the gear and headed home. I purchased a new bike because I did not want any potential maintenance issues, as I only wanted to ride not tinker with repairs.

I brought home the bike to Bowen Island and took some time to explore every nook and cranny on the island, both on-road and off-road leading up to the summer. I learned that going up on loose gravel may make the rear-wheel spin, but overall, I was impressed by the versatility of how the bike rode, and I did not have any serious mishaps. Then came my summer break and I boarded onto the Langdale ferry to head up to our cottage. On the way I decided to stop at a motocross park in Sechelt, just to try it. I was surprised to arrive at the park with not a soul in sight. Steep dunes, jumps, and sandy terrain lay ahead. I positioned the bike at the top of the hill and started down the course. The terrain had thick soft sand and with some meandering I made it to the top of the next hill and the one after. The next descent brought me to a roundabout with sand as thick and deep as a beach. As I rounded the corner, the bike dug into the trail and stalled in the mountains of sand. I pulled the bike out and fishtailed out of the sand dunes to the bottom of the motocross course. The only way out was to go back to where I had started, as there was no exit at the bottom. With a running start, I powered up the slope until I finally made it to the steepest part of the hill; and I managed to ride the bike over the ridge and back to freedom and normal roads. That was the only time I went to the sand dunes. After a rough start, the rest of the trip up to the cottage went smoothly, and once there I washed off all the sand from the bike.

Over the summer I explored backcountry-logging roads on the Sunshine Coast, very comfortable handling my bike. When the summer ended, I rode back to my dealer, where I sold back the bike having clocked 800 kilometers on it over the summer.

My new Yamaha 250XT road bike, 2018

Creative Expression

Hypnosis

Outside of my profession, I completed courses in Neuro-Linguistic Programming (NLP) and Hypnosis. A dentist I knew used hypnosis as part of his practice and claimed it to be very effective. Before I took a hypnosis course, I could not sleep one night and as I was tossing about, I turned to Geraldine who was dreaming and making some muffling sounds. I thought I would try to see if I could hypnotize her without having any training. I spoke to her very softly and asked her if she could hear me. She made some sounds indicating that she did. Next I told her that I would ask her to do some things for me. I asked her to raise her left hand into the air. She promptly put up her left hand. Next I asked her to put her left hand back down. She did so. I followed this up by asking her to raise her right hand straight up into the air, and she complied. Next I asked her to put back down her right arm, and it flopped back down. Encouraged by this compliance I then asked her to sit straight up and she sat bolt upright without a hint of being awake! I then asked for her to put both of her arms high up in the air, which she did. I was amazed. Finally, I asked her to put her arms back down, and she did and then I asked her to lie back down and have a deep restful sleep. She complied. It was clear she was completely unconscious throughout this whole episode. It was fascinating that this was possible to do this without any formal training!

I asked Geraldine if she remembered my commands, and she did not. Although the potential is limitless in this field, I have not pursued this further even after taking a hypnosis course.

Music

As a one-off, I decided to learn how to play "Greensleeves" on the piano. I first learned the basics using my Apple computer, and then when I had some basics down, went to Elaine, a piano teacher. The objective was to learn to play in time for Christmas. I practiced the piece and was soon able to play it by memory. Although this was a modest piano objective, it came in handy on a number of occasions. Once we were at Taliesin West in Scottsdale, Arizona and we took a tour of Frank Lloyd Wright's winter compound. The tour guide stopped in FLW's living room and described how FLW loved playing his Steinway. She then proceeded to ask if anyone would like to try the piano. I jumped at the chance and sat down while I had an audience of the US National Women's Soccer team who was part of the tour group. I proceeded to play the one piece I knew. After the applause I basked in my one modest musical recital.

Although I very much enjoy music, being a musician did not draw me when I was younger. I had too much energy and I wanted to use it up with sports. I also had more interest in the visual arts. In retrospect, I feel pursuing music would have been good too. I saw how a friend learned the trumpet and he was able to leverage this skill with interesting opportunities like playing at many functions, including Club Med; and he also met his wife at a gig while he was one of the "boys in the band."

Even though I did not pursue music, I put it on my 100 Life Visions to write at least one song, and acting as vocalist have it recorded. In the summer of 2016, I had a few days on my own at our cottage and I sat down to write my lyrics. After a few hours over three days, I had my first draft. I wrote about what I was passionate about and what I knew, namely, celebrating "Cottage Life." In the fall I approached Matt, a Juno-nominated guitarist, and he agreed to write the music to my lyrics. He had some good suggestions, one of which was to shorten words to fewer syllables. We agreed that since I wrote the lyrics, and he was creating the music, we would own the song 50-50. The goal was to have a recording ready by New Year's Eve, and we only had one week.

I went to his recording studio and found the process fascinating. Once the song was recorded to an acceptable level, it was only necessary to adjust or re-record parts of the song rather than the entire piece. Matt would then take the newly recorded piece and insert it using computer software into the song. If he asked me to re-sing the words "Cottage Life" louder than before it would be overwritten into the track. A professional back-up singer was hired for parts of the song. We had a finished version by year-end and three years later I loaded the song on to multiple music streaming services including Apple Music and Spotify.

Cottage Life

Misty air fades away
Morning shivers greet the new day
Calling loons dance when they awake
Sun rises golden on the lake
Maple syrup pancakes, coffee in the air
Crunching leaves and breath of a black bear
Embers glow to life in the fireplace
There is a smile on everybody's face

Cottage life we love to wake
By the dock at the lake
Happy hours on Muskoka chairs
Friends, living life, without a care

A friendly beaver swims by our canoe
Now we know what to do
Rope swing and dive into the clear water
Sun is shining it's getting hotter
In the hammock two of us can share
Telling secrets if we dare
Cottage chef busy making cottage treats
Come to the harvest table it's time to meet

Cottage life we love to be
Surrounded by all the beauty
Breathing in the country air
Living every moment - without a care

Stone hearth stories do abound
Table tennis with friends around
Mesquite smells and cocktail clatter
Dusk is unfolding at the lake
Porch rings with glasses and laughter
Boathouse retreat not long after
Now it's time for what truly matters
Live the life and love you want to make

Cottage life - where we want to be
Cottage life - come and see
Cottage life - where we want to be
Cottage life - feel so free

Cottage life we love to wake
By the dock at the lake
Happy hours on Muskoka chairs
Friends, living life, without a care
Cottage life we love to be
Surrounded by all the beauty
Breathing in the country air
Living every moment - without a care

Temple of Love

On January 28, 2018 I visited Château Versailles in France with my two daughters. We were on our way to drop off Francesca in Malta, where she studied for a semester and Selena came along for the ride.

Touring a fortress in Malta with Francesca and Selena, 2018

On the grounds of the château we walked to the "Petit Trianon," a charming village with English gardens. Here there is a beautiful Greek-inspired architectural folly called the "Temple of Love" built in 1778. It inspired me to build a Canadian version at our cottage. Upon returning home, I researched on Google Maps the width of the roof of the original structure. It is 36' and I then decided that a one-third scale, i.e. 12' diameter would be in proportional context for our property and project. I also found an elevation of the structure that allowed me to calculate the right proportions. The original structure has 12 pillars but scaling this to four would not work aesthetically or architecturally. Also, 12 columns would block too much light. I decided on eight pillars, as the right number to support the cupola roof and still be aesthetically pleasing. Since there are eight pillars in HEROISMS, it proved a delightful coincidence. In the original structure there is a formal diamond triangular pattern on the floor. I sought out more interesting Roman antique mosaics that would be in context with the "Temple of Love." After much research I discovered the Villa Romana del Casale in Sicily from the first quarter of the fourth century AD. The mosaics are beautifully detailed and constructed in small stone and marble pieces. The theme that inspired me is one of a couple embracing in a medallion format, which would be perfect for a circular floor plan. I found a company based in Turkey called "Mosaic Natural" with an office in New York that offered an artisan level of work to create custom mosaic medallions. Their initial quote was $7,500 US, which I told them did not meet my budget, however if they were to have a sale, to call me. The next day a representative called me to say that they would do the project for $5,200 US, and I agreed. The tiles would arrive in nine heavy four-foot rolls by courier.

"Temple of Love" at our cottage, 2019

The original structure has a marble statue of Cupid, which was chosen by Marie Antoinette, overriding her architect, who had a different statue in mind. The structure itself is an architectural folly, for no practical purpose other than as an element in a garden to enhance its beauty. For this purpose, it achieved its aim wonderfully.

A company from Kamloops, a town in the interior of BC, won the bid to create a complex roofing structure with over 1,000 pieces of cedar to achieve the cupola effect. For the eight posts, I cut the cedar logs from our two-acre property, of which half is wooded. I did not expect to be a logger on our own property, but since we had a good choice of cedar trees, it added to the experience to cut my own logs. I learned about cedar fungus considering two of the eight logs I had cut had three-inch rot at the base of the trees right at the heartwood. I cut another tree to get two more good posts without any fungus. I ordered a hand held log peeler from Québec and that proved efficient in peeling the bark, though with no shortage of sweat and the occasional peel of my skin. This was hard work, as I had to peel over uneven surfaces with knots. It required patience more than anything else. The logs then had to be debarked for the second time, sanded, washed and stained.

The site preparation included putting down crushed gravel, and building up retaining walls to allow a footpath around the outline of the structure. There were enough stones on the property to do this job. A Bobcat excavator created a flat 13' foot circular area on top of a granite cliff. We poured a concrete pad and installed it with the help of a pump truck since the aggregate had to go up a hill, where a leveler and placer were part of the team.

Photos of the mosaic were sent to me as they created the medallion. There were subtle changes going back and forth a few times with a beautiful end result and then it was installed before the statue arrived. To the mosaic creator's credit, they said they would fix any problems and were always accommodating to requests.

A carpenter was dispatched to construct our "Temple of Love." She was competent and it was impressive to watch her skills put to work. After seeing the complexity of the roof, I gained a new understanding for the delay in getting the forms with the many roofing pieces. The first job was to place curved beams onto the posts. She glued multiple pieces together to create the two layers of the beams. She then installed with a "T"-shaped anchor that she drilled into the base. She then cut and leveled the tops of the posts. The raising of the circular beams was risky but it worked and they were secured to each of the posts. The hard part was now done. The bracing was easy to rise and all six went smoothly. She installed 1,000 roofing pieces in preparation for the copper panels. The carpenter proceeded to sand the roof to give a perfect curve. Jose, the copper-roofer, came by and assessed the situation before he could do the work. At the apex of the ribs inside the roof, I placed a wood carved eagle crest, which served as homage to the original temple that also has an eagle crest at the same spot, and it is also appropriate in context of the bald eagles that swoop by on the lake.

The final touch was a statue custom-ordered in bronze. I chose Rodin's "The Bather" as an appropriate piece due to the lake connection. The sculpture was commissioned overseas and arrived in the summer ready to be installed on a plinth I had created in preparation for the 225-pound sculpture. The plinth came from a cedar tree that was cut down on Bowen Island in my neighbourhood. I asked the owner if it would be alright if I cut a piece. He agreed and the 300-pound round ended up being just the right size for the statue. I installed rollers on the bottom of the plinth so the sculpture could be moved back to the edge if we wanted the open space available for other uses. I rolled up the plinth on wool carpets to the temple and brought the statue up in a wheelbarrow in reverse. I was on my own so I had to do all the work. The statue worked out very well proportionally and aesthetically and this completed the project. I kept the statue a surprise for Geraldine for when I unveiled and dedicated the temple to her.

On this same trip to France we visited the medieval wonder of Notre-Dame de Paris that is truly magnificent. We walked up to the roof where the decaying worn stonework left you with the impression that the structure may collapse at any time. Fifteen months later a fire brought down the whole roof, so we saw it just in time.

Reading and Writing

I started writing in my journal at 26 and have kept it ever since, writing at a minimum monthly and often weekly and occasionally daily. My first contribution to a book was for the "Greater Vancouver Book" where I wrote about Bowen Island, the community I live in. HEROISMS was conceived in 2015 and after sporadic starts I decided in December 2018 that in 2019 I would finally complete a rough draft. I would be turning 57 in 2019 and at the time I noticed how accomplished people with heavy demands on their time like Dr. Jordan Peterson, a renowned psychologist, professor, and writer who is six weeks younger than me, has numerous writing credits; not to mention Stephen Harper who, while acting as Prime Minister of Canada, wrote a book about hockey. I had no excuse not to get this done, especially since two hours a day can be frittered away on non-productive endeavours in a heartbeat. This reminds me of the well-known rocks-in-the jar anecdote, where you should concentrate on the important things to put in a jar, the rocks, and then put pebbles in the crevices, the moderately important things, and then pour sand in the remaining areas that represent the least important things that should be minimized or delegated.

I accomplished the writing tasks through reverse engineering with a daily requirement of writing 1,000 words. Since I established a 50,000-word objective based on books that had a style and substance of the type I wanted to convey, this only required 50 days writing. With a few days off it was a task that could be accomplished in two months writing less than two hours a day. By time-blocking my writing in the evening and starting in the fall, I accomplished the task before my New Year's Eve deadline.

My fascination for "what is" focuses almost all of my reading on non-fiction, since life is full of facts more amazing than fiction. I do allow the occasional fiction book when it is a truly outstanding work, peer-reviewed to be the highest quality literature. Evelyn Waugh's "Brideshead Revisited" comes to mind. It is sobering to know that to read what you want may take several lifetimes. As my father started giving his 5,000-book library away in preparation for moving into a nursing home, I asked if he could give me "The Story of Civilization" by Will and Ariel Durant, an eleven-volume detailed look at history throughout the ages. With the many other reading demands, it usually takes me one year to complete one volume, so it is an 11-year plus exercise just to read these books. My father shared my non-fiction focus and I accepted about 200 books leaving many behind that, in retrospect, would have been great to own, including a 19th century edition of a landscape design book on Capability Brown.

Cottage Life

It was a year after high school that my father built a cedar log cabin near Stowe, Vermont. For the next decade I would often go there or to Bruce's "camp" at Bark Lake in Québec.

War canoes, regatta, Bark Lake, QC, 2009

To this day I cannot think of a better way to spend time with family, friends, or even on your own. Monks have figured this out as they often have retreats separate from their main residence. Elements of British society have a long tradition of owning a country house along with a home in London. No matter how pleasant your main residence, there is something rejuvenating about having another place to go in a natural environment, and away from the cacophony of the city and its daily routine. In my twenties I would on occasion go with friends to be part of the vibrant Montreal nightlife, but even then I preferred to go to the country given a choice. Through a lifetime of experience, I find social gatherings ranging from two to six to be optimal and if they take place in a cottage environment - that is the best!

If there were one example of persistence in my life, finding a lakefront property would be it. After Geraldine and I moved to Vancouver, we no longer had the easy access of going to my family's country place. Vermont and the charm of its villages was a wonderful place to go and enjoy time away from the urban life in Montreal. When I lived in Toronto, I would make it a point to get back there although it was a long trip to make just for a weekend. When we moved out to the West Coast and started a family, I only made two more trips to Vermont before my parents sold the property in 2006. Ever since we moved to Vancouver in 1991, I had spent time researching and looking for a country getaway. There were a number of false starts in finding one. First, on Nelson Island we had an accepted offer on a waterfront lot that was stunningly beautiful, but it would have pushed our finances too much at the time, so we had to let it go. Then we found and purchased a lot at Deka Lake in the interior of BC. It was not the ideal vision since it was not on the water, and when we needed the funds it was sold. Later I found two lots on Stuart Lake that we purchased, a one-and-a-half-hour drive from Prince George and it was so remote that it was more of a hunter-trapper cabin setup and not ideal for the family. It was sold within a year for a 100% gain so not all was lost. Next we put in an offer with a friend on the Sunshine Coast on Sakinaw Lake, where there was a cottage on a half-acre island. It was a charming cottage but limited by the size of the island, and as well as being water access. Also, it was a very windy spot that on certain days would make it a challenge to get to. We made an offer and came close to an agreement but did not chase the price and let it go. Next, another six-acre island with a cottage on Ruby Lake came up and the expense of buying it at the time made it only feasible by having multiple partners. We had an accepted offer and I structured a quarter share arrangement that in theory would work but, in the timeframe allowable I was not able to get the ideal partners in place, so we let that opportunity go.

Finally, in 2010 after 19 years, we bought a two-acre lakefront property on the Sunshine Coast. We rented on nearby Sakinaw Lake for years and continually kept a lookout for places for sale. On one summer family holiday a real estate agent said, "If you want lakefront, look at this place. I would buy it if I had the funds." I was up early the next morning and before anyone else awoke, I drove to the address the agent gave me. I arrived to see a "For Sale" sign, but there was no indication of waterfront, and all I saw was an overgrown country road going into the forest. I thought to myself that we were looking for a place to swim on a lake and not looking to go logging! I turned around and went back to the vacation rental. I called the agent and said, "I went to the property, but I did not see waterfront and so I left." He replied, "No, that is it. There is a private road that winds its way down to the lake." This time as a family, we jumped into our minivan and drove back to the property and down a road with tall grass. Sure enough, after passing a wooden shed the road descended towards a lake with the water shimmering through the trees. We parked and made our way down to the lake on an overgrown path and walked on to a dock that was made of planks of wood on two floating logs. It was wonderful and offered complete solitude surrounded by large tracts of forest. We put on our bathing suits and jumped off the dock. We knew then that the long search was over and this would be it. As we left, Selena, said, "It is a beautiful lake, but there is one problem; there is no cottage." We all laughed.

I called the listing agent to put in an offer right away. I was surprised I did not know the property since I had thoroughly researched lakefront places and the property had been on the market for months. I looked on the online real estate listings in the area, clicked on waterfront and still, the property did not come up. I looked further and eventually found it! The agent had made an error and classified it under bare land without specifying waterfront. Anyone searching for waterfront would not have seen it in the listings! There were two errors: 1. The sign on the road did not specify waterfront and 2. The property was misclassified online.

When we closed the deal, the agent said he had wondered why it had taken so long to sell. I knew why. After the closing a young woman and her friends came down the road, and she introduced herself. Coincidentally she was the daughter of the owner of the cottage we were renting on a nearby lake. She said it was her dream to buy the property we had found and that she had been looking at it for months and was lining up a friend to buy it together. The agent called her and told her of our offer and if she still wanted the place, she would need to place a competing offer right away. She declined since she could not act so fast. We all learn from experience and hopefully in due time, she was able to find her own piece of paradise. The learning lesson is if you want something:

Line up the ducks in advance so you can act like a lightning bolt when the opportunity strikes.

On the very first free weekend after the purchase I went up on my own for a day to clear the road of overgrowth. I purchased a weed whacker and blazed away for five hours. The constant twisting motion did not bother me until that evening when my

Geraldine on the day we found our lakefront property, 2010

knees became inflamed, and later I had I learned that I had caused damage to the ligaments. It took a full two years to fully recover from this. The takeaway is to read the manual for weed whackers and rather than twist your legs, instead move your hips in a way to not cause strain on your knees. Another lesson is to limit repetitive activity like this to short lengths of time. A good part of the two-acre property was overgrown with impassable woods, large log piles, and both standing forest and uprooted trees. In exploring the property, it was a real surprise to come across a pipe sticking out of the ground with a tap on it. When I turned on the tap, high-pressure water came out. In the wilderness lot we were on a municipal water system and it was working! Over the next four years we lived on the property by renovating a small shed into a guest cottage or Bunkie along with a newer 26' trailer the seller donated. Bears were a common sight, along with many other wildlife including deer, raccoons, bald eagles, beavers, coyotes, and the endangered painted-back turtle. The turtles often make their way up from the lake to our road and lay their eggs there. This is not the most ideal spot, and I invited up a wilderness conservation group to discuss a turtle breeding area on the property. For the next four years we swam in the pristine warm lake, built a new dock, and created trails through the woods. We were able to find lot lines reasonably easily since a survey was done in the not too distant past and they were well marked. We enjoyed the property for three summers, while we planned to build a cottage, a major item on my 100 Life Visions.

After feeling-out the property and recognizing where the sunrays landed, we were ready for the next step to prepare the site for a cottage. The best decision we made, although expensive, was to bring in a landscape designer to optimize the site for the future cottage and landscaping. The site manipulation was extensive and the charming woodsy lot looked like a moonscape after excavators came in and started clearing the site. At one-point Kerry, the excavator operator, called me to say there is was a large, spherical boulder right where we were planning a badminton court. It looked like the one in *Raiders of the Lost Ark*. He asked, "What do you want to do with this?" I said, "Roll it away onto the shore of the lake." He replied, "The excavator is not able to do this so you only have one option – to dynamite it." After this the site preparation started to take shape. I was quoted $2,000 to burn a pile of branches and logs. It seemed like a good cost savings to simply go up and burn it myself with some matches and kindling. When I came up and saw the pile, it was as large as a house with logs four feet thick. It ended up being carted away. I instructed the landscaper to prepare the site below where the cottage was going to be built with the idea that this way we could work backwards and therefore would not have to disturb the area near the lake after the cottage was built. This was a good idea, as when we came up after the site preparation was complete, we could not believe our eyes. It looked like our place had been transformed into a botanical garden.

We hired a log and timber frame designer, and I proceeded to interview builders. I showed the plans to a builder and his partner and I asked if they were capable of building a 2,800 sq. ft. cottage for $400,000 without finishing the basement. He looked at the plans intensely and said, "It is tight but I will be able to do this." After the project was underway, two months into it, I asked the builder if we were on track financially. He said, "We will keep building until you run out of money and then we will pull the crew." He failed to mention this before getting the contract! Nonetheless he completed the build right on time one year after the landscaping was done and five months after the project began. It was not on budget however as the costs ended up being $500,000, plus another $200,000 to finish the lower level since we had decided to do that as well. It ended up being a $700,000 build. The building inspector commented on the quality of construction, remarking that the house was "built like a rock" - exactly what we wanted. As a symbolic gesture, I used my portion of a pre-inheritance for the foundation, as I know my parents would have liked this. My brother Denis, inspected the foundation, and Lori and Bill contributed to our projects as well, so there was multiple family input.

An interesting feature of West Coast cottages, or "cabins" as they are often referred to here, is that you do not see screened-in porches like you would see in East Coast cottages. This is due to the lack of bugs, which do not require the screens. In the summer, bugs prefer to procreate in hot, humid environments, rather than the hot, dry climate like you would experience on the West Coast

Cottage foundations, Sunshine Coast, 2014

Would we do something differently if done over again? Yes, but not because we are not happy with what we built, as we are. Before we built, a neighbour's home adjoining our property on the non-waterfront side came up for sale for $260,000; it was a nice functional home with a quarter acre of land. If we had bought then we would have instantly had a home and expanded our lot, and then we could have still had built a nice, smaller log cabin on the lake and it would have fit into our budget. For $660,000 we would have had two homes, increased our acreage, and had a caretaker's residence.

Now that the cottage is built and our daughters are adults, they take their own friends up to enjoy the lake. Soon we may expand by another generation to extend memories there.

Cottage completed, Sunshine Coast, 2014

Canoe Trip on Forest Lake Loop

In 2016 I decided to seek out more adventures. I emailed a few friends to see who would be interested in canoeing a five-day Powell River Forest Canoe loop on the Sunshine Coast. I figured this would work best with a group of two or four. Initially there were three takers but two backed out and it ended up being John and I. Since John lives on the Sunshine Coast, it worked great to organize the trip. The starting point was at our family's cottage where the night before the trip we heard a cougar attack on a mother deer and her two fawns. We saw the deer while it was still bright and the attack took place later in the dark. The muffled sounds of the rolling attack were close to the cottage but in the woods where there are no paths. After that wildlife adventure, the next morning we loaded my 60 lb. Chestnut canoe onto John's truck and off we went to take the ferry from Egmont to Saltery Bay. I had organized in advance a pick-up at the destination spot on Powell Lake where we left the truck and the driver drove us to the starting point a half-hour from the town of Powell River. The weather was great. He loaded up the canoe and off we went. We camped four nights and portaged between eight lakes. One of the lakes was artificially raised so we canoed through a forest on top of the trees, a surreal experience. We met very few people on the trip and the portaging between lakes followed a well-organized trail with canoe rests that allowed one person to carry a canoe for 100 metres before it could be lowered on to the rests and the second person could take over. We would switch back and forth without an interruption. An ingenious system not unlike when you lift weights, where after a set and a brief break, you can again do another set, again and again.

We came across an ancient massive cedar stump that had been hollowed out and had a roof put on top; an outhouse had been constructed on the inside, something a hobbit would appreciate. On the flooded forest we once became stuck on top of a tree just below the water line. This in an area where there was not a soul. If the canoe tipped, we would be on our own and without cellular service. To dislodge the canoe from the top of the tree, I pushed a paddle on to the tree that jerked the canoe enough to dislodge but not enough to tip. The last portage included a steep downhill section where it was awkward to carry the canoe and too steep to carry it up on your shoulders. We took either end and carried it that way or slid it down the path in the steepest sections.

Powell Lake was the final waterway on the trip, and it was an open water long, open water excursion to our campsite. The wind often picks up on this lake, creating whitecaps, which would force us to seek shelter on shore. We were fortunate not to have significant waves, and we paddled to our final evening destination in warmth for half an hour before the sunshine left the campsite. John was a great paddling partner and meticulously organized with his gear and food preparations. We celebrated the end of the trip at a pub with a well-deserved beer. I was sore for a while recovering from carrying a heavy canoe on my shoulders, but it was not onerous and proved the right challenge to push me though not beyond my limits. A lighter canoe would have made the trip much easier; however, I already had the Chestnut and it worked well too. We fast-tracked this trip so we completed it in four nights instead of five. This was helped by the great weather and our willingness to push on.

Travel

Expanding horizons beyond your community and country offers fresh perspectives and helps avoid falling into the trap of being provincial. I was 21 on my first travel outside of North America when I did a "Let's Go Europe"-type holiday. I never looked back as I enjoy the cultural differences and challenge to the normal way one does things by being in the midst of other nations. If you are fortunate enough to have the ability to take on a second citizenship, this can be an effective way to experience and even live and work in other countries. An EU passport, as an example, not only opens the world to Europe but also some Caribbean islands and even some in the South Pacific. If one takes on a second citizenship it allows your children to take on their own dual citizenship, which they may use if the opportunity arises. An EU citizenship may be purchased for anyone who does not qualify through family. Certain countries like Malta sell their passports to get into the EU, although the price is steep, costing more than $1 million US at the time of this writing.

Consider meaningful travel to contribute to the world in some way that combines international living with volunteer work to pursue a community goal, e.g. Roadscholar (play on Rhodes Scholar), Habitat for Humanity, and Doctors without Borders.

Excellent resources for planning a trip include National Geographic's "Destinations of a Lifetime." By reviewing the ideas in the book you can place yellow stickies on the ideas you like and you then plan a life of adventures – just with this one book! If you wish to live internationally, then <u>International Living</u> is a great resource that highlights opportunities around the world.

When planning trips where the most agreeable weather is a consideration, look at areas that include: Canary Islands, Kenya, Hawaii, Costa Rica, Bermuda, Mexico City, San Paulo, Southern Spain, Southern France, Malta, Italy, and San Diego.

Ensure that your passport, birth certificate, and identification have your name written in exactly the same way. A discrepancy may cause problems at customs. My passport was washed in the laundry, which impacted the colour quality of my photo. A customs official in Asia said that they would allow this but are not required to accept it.

Keep a clear record of your shots to prevent having to do too many unnecessarily and also to save on the costs. Getting shots recently for my family of four costs over $1,000 for a trip to Asia. Were they all necessary? Maybe, maybe not, but it is better to be safe than sorry. Even with all of these shots we all became sick anyway!

Split money, credit cards, and other travel documents into two separate stacks and store them separately. If one is lost, the other stash should suffice. Changing currency should be done in official areas and not through unauthorized persons. I once changed US dollars, the currency used in Cambodia, at a coffee shop. I was given back a fake $50 US bill as part of my change. An annoying lesson to learn.

Going forward I look forward to more physically challenging nature adventures. The way I see it, even when you are 90, you can do more sedentary holidays like bus tours or cruises but there is a time span for the more physically challenging trips that should be experienced sooner than later. The average person declines in health at age 72, according to some studies. This is perhaps the best reason not to wait to plan too long for your retirement. I sidestepped potentially more serious issues when I had stents put into my arteries. Now I do not take anything for granted and strive to be effective with each and every day, pursuing meaningful activities whether at work or in my free time.

When inviting friends on a travel adventure, find the right companion who is both capable and a good personality-fit to spend a week or longer together.

Elephant sanctuary, Chiang Mai, 2019

Tracking the places that you visit helps identify where else one may wish to go. I listed the countries I visited in Appendix C.

With decades of lifetime travels there were many wonderful experiences I had that fortunately sidestepped setbacks. I will describe here three travel situations where everything did *not* go as planned.

137

Pope John Paul II at the Vienna Airport

In the summer of 1983 when I was finishing my first trip to Europe, I was in Vienna visiting a college acquaintance who worked at the United Nations. Years later, I would find out my father-in-law, Bill Brind, a well-known documentary filmmaker had also worked in that building. After a tour of the UN and on my way to the Vienna airport, I carried with me three-foot-long salami that I thought would be a good gift to bring back home to my parents in Canada. I had it wrapped in brown paper and placed it horizontally on top of my shoulder luggage. As I entered the airport two soldiers with machine guns came up to me, pointed their weapons, and directed me to walk towards a security gate. The long tube had alerted them to a potential risk. When I arrived at the metal scanners, they asked me to place the luggage on a conveyor belt and only after it cleared security did they lower machine guns, turn around and leave. After I went through security, I looked outside and on the tarmac standing at the door of his airplane was Pope John Paul II waving to a crowd below. He was in Vienna for celebrations marking 300 years since the victory of Christian European armies against the attacking Ottoman Muslim forces. Security was at a heightened level, and it was not the best day to be transporting a long cylinder through an international airport lobby. To top it off I flew to New York where I had a stop over, and when I arrived at customs they confiscated the salami, as passengers were not allowed to transport certain food products over the US border. I was only 21 and a lesson was learned.

Blizzard on the Icefield's Parkway

In the spring of 1987 I was looking for summer work in Jasper and I set my hopes on being a white-water rafting guide. While waiting to find out if I had a position that I had applied for, I headed to Banff a 287-km drive away. I left Jasper on a sunny day and drove on the magnificent highway that rises in elevation to 2,085 metres. It started to snow, and snow and snow as I approached the Columbia Icefields Glacier 142 kilometers from Jasper and about half way to Banff. The snow turned to a blizzard and the speed of the snowflakes hitting my windshield created a surreal lightshow effect with no visibility of the road ahead. Going very slowly was not a problem, but the call of nature proved otherwise. I realized I could not make it to Jasper without a rest stop, and with the mountains of snow around me there was no great place to stop. I pulled over the best I could along the steep road and put my van into park. There was a cliff to my right so my only option was to leave the van to avoid being caught short while I stood on the snow-covered highway with almost no visibility. As I stood in the blizzard in my golf shirt and shorts, I glanced at my van and to my shock I saw it slowly starting to slide backward. I had to make a split-second decision: If I jumped back into the van I could steer it away from the edge of the cliff and hopefully stop it before the vehicle went over, or I could let the van go over the cliff and find a way to survive in the snow storm before another car passed by. Although challenging myself to see how I could survive in a windswept blizzard would be an interesting exercise to see if I could foster some ingenuity to do so, I elected the former option and I jumped back in the van, applied the brake and slid to a stop. After catching my breath, I continued on my journey and as I descended towards

Banff, the weather relaxed to more of a normal snowfall and I was able to drive to a truck stop, thankful how things turned out. Coincidentally, while I was editing the final draft of this book there was accident in the vicinity where I had my incident and with tragic outcomes of an all-terrain bus rolling over with three fatalities.

Marooned on Jedediah Island

There is a beautiful 600-acre island in the Georgia Straight that was owned by a couple from Seattle, from 1949 to 1994. With mountains, old growth forests, orchards, fresh water, fields and multiple coves, it is simply amazing that this island, larger than the country of Monaco, was a cottage property for only two people. In the early '90 the couple approached the government of British Columbia and said they had had an offer to buy the island for $15 million. They said that the island should instead be a marine park and if the government would give them $4 million, then they could have it at the substantially discounted price. The government agreed to pay half if the public would fundraise for the other half. This took place, and the island is now available for day trips. I put it on my 100 Life Visions to sail to this island. Since my brother-in-law Brandon my had a sailboat, we, along with a crew, headed up to the island on a warm day in July.

We anchored in a deep, east-facing, protected cove where we went for the briefest of swims since the water was very cold even in the summer. Brandon and I decided to explore the coastline and island and we left the crew with the sailboat and went by dinghy on smooth flat water to a cove at the west side of Jedediah. We hiked through the forest and then noticed that the tops of the trees were swaying in the wind. A storm was coming. We

Sailing to Jedediah Island, 2009

headed back to the dinghy and hugged the shoreline in now choppy waves with whitecaps. In the distance we could see lightning and hear thunder, a rare occurrence on the West Coast. As we turned into the protected, cove the sailboat was gone. It had had to leave due to the danger of the wind striking the hull against the rock walls. We thought we would see if we could go back out and find the sailboat, but the waves were so high we headed back to shore. Now wet and with nightfall coming we had to plan to hunker down on this remote island without any services. Fortunately, Brandon had a flashlight that gave off a red strobe in case anyone was looking for us. We flipped the dinghy upside down above the high-water mark and planned to sleep under it, marooned on this rocky island. The strobe light was put on top of the boat so if another boat came into the cove, they would see us.

Marooned on Jedediah Island, 2009

Meanwhile we found out later that the crew on the sailboat had called the coast guard to pick us up. An aluminum, heavy duty coast guard boat saw the flashing red beacon and came into the cove, and in pitch darkness we tied up the dinghy to the back of the boat and we were taken out to meet the sailboat.

CHAPTER EIGHT

SOCIETY – OUR INTERCONNECTEDNESS

"In order to make a difference, we have to be willing to leave our comfort zones. In doing so, we start to struggle. It's in the struggle that we're given the opportunity to tap our reserves. This is when we see our personal best – in the struggle. The conquest lies in penetrating those barriers of self-imposed limitations and getting through to that good stuff – the stuff called potential, 90% of which we rarely use."

Sharon Wood

Olympics and Paralympics

In 1973 when I was 11, the Royal Bank of Canada sponsored a Junior Olympics program in my community of Montreal West to introduce youth to the spirit of the Olympic games. I

143

enthusiastically participated in field hockey and was delighted to get a certificate for this experience. This was the beginning of my affection for competitive sport and the Olympic games. I also have an Olympic family connection as a distant cousin Gabor Boronkay, was a FIFA official in the 1928 Amsterdam Olympics, and an uncle of mine trained as pentathlon athlete who, if he had not died as soldier in WWII, may have been a candidate for his national team.

Montreal 1976

As a young teenager I watched with great interest the construction of Montreal's Olympic Stadium with all its construction delays, labour, and engineering problems. For years this was the top news item and I followed it intensely. I lined up as soon as tickets became available for the public, though I was surprised to see how few events were available. I watched the opening ceremonies on television and noticed how many young kids took part of the performance celebrations. I thought, *why did not anyone tell me you could do this?* I would have jumped at the chance, as at the time I was far too young to even approach competing in a national level sport for these games. No doubt my passion for the Olympic movement was fostered from my hometown having hosted the games. I maintained a special fondness for both the competition and the ceremonies. In actuality, my first recollection of the Olympics came from the previous games in 1972 when I was 10, and I watched the athletes walking into the Munich stadium on a television with fuzzy reception. It was the same year my parents separated.

Calgary 1988

My focused sport volunteer involvement started with the 1988 Calgary Winter Olympic Games, where I signed up to work in the media centre as a host and offer help on using the email systems. I left my job at CP as I was looking for a new experience and the Olympics were a good break before my next career move. Arriving in Calgary opened the door to a new world of an international community, which was a refreshing complement to my career, and I enjoyed the experience immensely. The gathering of athletes from around the world, unified in a celebration of sport and culture, was unique in that it was an event that focused on humanity working together as opposed to the more common conflicts that we are exposed to in the media. For me a highlight of the games was occurred when my supervisor offered me a ticket to go the athletes' party at the end of the games. That moment stood out, confirming to me that this organization was one I would like to support and get involved with further. I already decided that focusing my energies was the right thing to do, but after the games were over, it was not clear what shape this would take. I called the Canadian Olympic Association (COA), now called the Canadian Olympic Committee (COC) to see if I could contribute in some way. There was no immediate opportunity, and it was clear that another approach would be needed.

Olympic Academy of Canada 2004

Olympic Academy of Canada, I am at the front right, Calgary, 2004

In 2004 I read about the Olympic Academy of Canada (OAC) a leadership development conference that congregates to hold workshops surrounding high performance sport. I enthusiastically applied and was put on a waiting list. I did not want to miss this so I responded by writing another letter on why I would be an excellent delegate. This worked and I was accepted to go to the one-week conference in Calgary and Banff.

When you ask for something and you do not have initial success, it does not necessarily mean forever. The timing may be off, and asking again, always politely, at a different time or in a different way or with someone else may work the second time.

This experience was a refreshing break from my practice and allowed me to expand my horizons without pressure on finances since the motivation was to make a difference and find new opportunities to contribute to the movement. Two major ideas came from this academy: 1. It was not too late for me to do something in sport as an athlete and see what I can accomplish, and 2. My new contacts in sport may allow for volunteer opportunities at the board level. I set out and accomplished both. I was also introduced to the Paralympics, which was also very interesting. Contacts led to an invitation to serve on the board of the Canadian Paralympic Foundation (CPF), my first step into organization in sports. I set it as one of my goals to compete internationally in sport as my last kick at the can to do so. I felt that I should do so if I was going to get involved in sport at organizational levels.

I approached the CPF and I was appointed as a director. I felt I had made a real difference there for the three years that I was involved. Through a contact at the Toronto Stock Exchange I was able to make an introduction that resulted in a $400,000 donation to the benefits of Paralympic curling. I was also curling at the time with a team grooming for international competition. The successes at the CPF lead me to run for Finance Director at the Canadian Paralympic Committee (CPC). I won the election, and this led into a different world, where politics were everywhere.

Torino 2006

It was wonderful being invited as a foundation board member to see my first Paralympics. I watched curling and skiing, and the setting of the closing ceremonies outside the Palazzo Madama and associated light show were stunningly beautiful. Another highlight was when I went up to Sestriere with a Canadian delegation that included an Ottawa senator. The day was splendid with great snow, a sunny and warm atmosphere, and the ideal combination for skiing. As we arrived at our seating, I learned that the Paralympic skiers were going to train on a nearby run. I decided that I was not going to sit there and only see the last few seconds of skiers coming down the mountain on a day that beautiful, and I wanted to go join the skiers on their training run! I excused myself from our group, rented some skis and headed up the chairlift. The breathtaking conditions, the fabulous air, and skiing with the athletes made this one of the most memorable ski days in my life. After a few hours I arrived back at the base of the mountain and met up with my group. One of the members came up to me and said, "When you left our group to go ski, I really wanted to join you but I felt I had to stay." Even though it was one amazing ski day, I downplayed it so she did not feel badly, replying, "It was interesting to ski with the Paralympians on their training runs."

"Life is not a spectator sport"

Jackie Robinson

Beijing 2008

Before I was elected to be the Finance Director at the CPC, I was invited to Beijing as a guest of the International Paralympic Committee (IPC). I arrived at the city's international airport, and while walking out I spoke to John Furlong the president of the Vancouver Organizing Committee (VANOC) for the 2010 Winter Olympic Games who had been on my flight. He kindly offered me a lift to my hotel, but I told him that I already had a driver waiting for me. In retrospect I should have taken the opportunity to learn more from behind the scenes leading up to 2010. Then with little delay I headed to the Bird's Nest stadium for the opening ceremonies. The air was so thick and humid that it was difficult to breathe, but the spectacular show and celebration of athletes more than made up for any discomfort. The initial feeling of Beijing was similar to a scene in the science fiction film *Blade Runner*, with steam coming out of grates, surrounded by rain and darkness. This completely changed when it became sunny with no obvious pollution in the air. There were so many venues to see, including invitations to Austria House, meeting Canadian athletes, the Hungarian Embassy, and visits to the Great Wall and the Forbidden City. At the Hungarian Embassy, as you walked up to the building, you were met with a row of younger Chinese women, immaculately dressed in white, who greeted you fluently in Hungarian.

Near the Great Wall at Badaling there is an elegant community of homes, one of which is used as a restaurant. There, a server wearing a black hat with a red communist star presented us with a wine list that included bottles as expensive as $1,500. This seemed like an unusual form of communism.

Walking the Great Wall of China, 2008

Heading to the Forbidden City proved a memorable start to the day. When I walked towards the line-up to enter the castle, an official saw my games accreditation around my neck and motioned that I should walk towards the grand doors, as I did not have to wait in line. As I approached the colossal gate, they opened up and I walked into the Forbidden City on my own. It was quite an experience to be in the palatial courtyards by myself.

The CPC was a completely different experience of running in an election contrasted from serving as a director at the CPF. At the foundation level, the work was mostly about finding funding for the athletes, while at the CPC oversaw activities related to the high-performance

With Princess Margriet of the Netherlands, Beijing, 2008

athletes with disabilities. Politics were much more apparent here, but nevertheless, it was good to be able to contribute, and I served my term.

In the subsequent election in 2009 I was up against one of Canada's most celebrated Paralympians who was also in the financial field, and he won that election. Just as well, as this was when I found out I needed to have an angioplasty. The Paralympic involvement led me to be appointed as a B Member, now called Supporter, of the COC in 2009, which I remain at the time of the writing.

With Dick Pound, IOC vice-president, 2008, Vancouver. He is a great role model in how to achieve competence in multiple disciplines.

Vancouver 2010

Leading up to these games I co-chaired a Gold Medal Plates fundraiser for athletes where Olympians were partnered with a chef, and guests had the opportunity to both meet athletes and dine on fabulous culinary creations. I also chaired the first "Paralympics Dreams Event" at UBC. For the games I decided I would like to contribute in three areas: attaché for a visiting country as suggested by an IOC member, opening or closing ceremonies, and international protocol. This partly worked and it partly did not. Arranging an attaché role was a chess game unto itself. Speaking Hungarian meant that, logically I could do this for Hungary. After many discussions the Consul General to Hungary in Vancouver told me, "I arranged it, you are attaché for Hungary." Great, except that nothing in writing arrived, and for the games a Hungarian Consul General from the US flew up for the games and took on the attaché role, overriding the local consul general. Considering that the attaché is supposed to be someone with local knowledge to help the team as needed, it was disappointing and not the last time in my life politics would get in the way. I put my name forward for a couple of other countries including the US to be an attaché. I spoke to the United States Olympic Committee and the local consul-general. They said they decided not to fill the attaché role since they already had sufficient resources. Later at a social function the US consul general was there and he approached me and said, "Hi Peter. How are you? We see that you also gave your name to other countries for the attaché role." Who were the 'we' exactly and how do they know?" Any inquiries I had made to National Olympic Committees were independent of each other. This is the new world order we live in. If you put your name forward to volunteer for a sporting event, your name may show up in a special opps cyber communications database. I can see why my mentor in wealth management choses to live a life as a hermit.

I did get a role for the Closing Ceremonies and took part in a life-sized rod hockey game. The rehearsals were frequent and the time commitment was massive, though it was fascinating to see the level of organization that took place. This was also a chance to bring to fruition a teenage aspiration of being part of an Olympic ceremony when I had missed my chance in Montreal.

Years later, another Olympic opportunity arose when Budapest applied to host the 2024 Olympic and Paralympic Games. I was approached by the local consul general for Hungary to see if I would be interested in serving as an ambassador for these games. I gathered my being located in North America may have been a useful contact for the bid committee leading up to 2024. Then the Hungarian government abruptly cancelled their bid and once again politics was involved, and Paris went on to win the right to host these games. Since Hungary or central Europe never had an Olympics, I think they were a strong candidate to win, especially since Hungary has the second highest medal count per capita, and the country was one of the founding members of the International Olympic Committee (IOC) and the modern Olympic games.

My second volunteer job was with International Protocol. The training was interesting as it included workshops from both the Canadian Security Intelligence Service (CSIS) and the IOC (International Olympic Committee). The year prior, I had written an article to the IOC on a request they had put out looking for material. See Appendix E.

With Jacques Rogge, IOC President, 2009

Compared to the ceremonies group, International Protocol seemed surprisingly disorganized. To top this off, my experience in that role was cut short since I unknowingly had sat beside the Crown

With HRH Prince Albert of Monaco, Vancouver 2010

Prince of Denmark while I was assigned to a New Zealand dignitary who was on the other side of me at a speed skating event. This was a problem, but who knew? I was apparently supposed to wait in another area while the skating took place. I was given a heads up that this position may end if I went to a meeting to discuss this, implying that I may not want to go. I decided to go anyway, partly since this would be the only time in my life I would be removed from a position and I wanted to see what this felt like, and I could learn more about what took place. The irony of this experience was that this was for a volunteer position and one that I gave my heart and soul to. I received a call shortly after from the New Zealand delegation assuring me they had nothing to do with this, as I was doing a great job for them. I think this is why I enjoy the entrepreneurialism of my profession where I have significant freedom to manage affairs in the way I see best for my clients without being confined in a box.

Later I received a call from the organizing committee offering me the same international protocol role for the Paralympics. Possibly this was to make up for the Olympics. I declined, as I had seen enough of this part of the of the games; although, I decided not to let this stop my enthusiasm for my other volunteer position and I successfully completed my role in the closing ceremonies.

"Be careful what you wish for."

Anonymous

After the games an Olympic museum was set up at the Richmond Olympic Oval and there was a call for donations. I gave the museum the hockey outfit I wore during the closing ceremonies, which established a positive association between the venue and myself. A decade later another good association took place at the same venue when I attended a COC function where a skating event was part of an evening social. I was the first person to step on the ice and there was a disk jockey at the side of the rink streaming music for the entire facility. I asked him to play the song I wrote, "Cottage Life." He pulled up the song, turned up the volume, and I sang along while I skated at full speed on the fresh ice and cool air. It was a delightful few minutes.

An especially memorable time during the games was when I was invited to USA House in Whistler. As you entered the large log home you were met by two chefs from Chicago who greeted you with, "Welcome to USA House, we are here to make your culinary dreams come true. You let us know what you would like us to make for you and we will create something special." What an entrance. The evening included athletes passing their medals around and likely discussion. I brought two guests with US ties with me who still talk about that evening a decade later.

If something negative happens to you, look for ways to turn it around to become a positive.

155

Another personal objective I had for the 2010 Winter Olympics and Paralympics was to ensure that both of my daughters took part in some volunteer capacity. They were too young to get involved for the Olympic ceremonies due to insurance limitations; however, the Paralympics

Selena, Francesca, and friend Helena wearing their 2010 Paralympic Opening Ceremonies outfits

allowed them to participate in the Opening Ceremonies, which they enjoyed immensely.

Meeting a US President

A letter arrived for me in the mail from the United States Secret Service. What do you do when you get a letter from them? You open that letter first! The letter said that I was invited to meet President Bill Clinton at a function at the Westin Hotel in downtown Vancouver in October of 2007. The invitation stemmed from a friend, Frank, at the Vancouver Board of Trade and was related to my involvement in sport. I was cleared by the secret service and through their correspondence where it said, "<u>You must bring this letter with you or there will be no access to the premises.</u>" On the day of the event I walked over to the hotel, just a few minutes from my office. As I approached the hotel, security was everywhere. There was a row of black SUV's with tinted windows, and many secret service dressed in suits walking around outside.

Their earpieces made it clear who they were. Once I entered the main entrance to the hotel, I walked inside and arrived at what looked like a security guard convention. There were hundreds of secret service staff. I went up an escalator and met a rotunda on top where a complete circle of security guards stood side-by-side looking at anyone coming up the escalator. As I stepped off the escalator, I walked up to a sign that showed where the various conference rooms were located. I identified the room on my invitation and walked down a corridor, again passing security people the entire way to two doors of the appropriate room. Two large secret service men stood on either side of the door, looking straight ahead. As I walked towards the doors, both security guards opened them for me and there, standing with six people in a huddle, was Bill Clinton. I thought it odd that there was no formal introduction so I joined the group as the former president was entrenched in the middle of a political discussion. A few minutes went by when a lady came into the room, tapped me on the shoulder, and whispered, "Excuse me, are you here for the Bill Clinton VIP function?" I said, "Yes, and I have the invitation letter." She said smiling, "That function starts in fifteen minutes. This is Mr. Clinton's private breakfast meeting." Sure enough, I saw a table with orange juice and croissants. I then walked out to an adjoining room where there was a reception, and soon after, a formal introduction. Considering the letter from the secret service and the hundreds of security people, and I was still without any problem, able to walk into Clinton's breakfast meeting. I must have looked like I belonged.

With President Bill Clinton, Vancouver, 2007

TEDx Abbotsford

In 2006 I was asked to give a brief speech at a Rona home improvement store on behalf of the CPF, since Rona was a sponsor of the 2010 Olympics and Paralympics. Although I was able to do it, my speech was not optimal and I realized I needed to up my game on public speaking. My brother Denis, who was a member of Toastmasters, encouraged me to join. I researched the clubs in Vancouver that suited my time schedule in the middle of the day and went to six different clubs as a guest. I chose Cloverleaf Toastmasters who met at the People's Law School near the Justice Institute. The caliber of the club and its speakers was high, and they also had the oldest Toastmaster in the world, Dr. Ralph Yorsh, who lived until he was 99 and still a member of the club until he passed away. He was a dentist and a number of his patients were members of the club. The ongoing joke was that his dental practice was a front for recruiting members to Toastmasters. Over the five years of being a member I obtained my DTM (Distinguished Toastmaster) designation. This was a relatively quick progression through the many levels and was made possible with a focused intent of achieving this goal. The time commitment was significant however, and after I accomplished this, I pulled back to concentrate more on the growth of my wealth management practice. I made it a point while travelling to drop in to other clubs, and I did so in places like Barbados, Scottsdale, and Las Vegas. I also had the opportunity to volunteer at an international Toastmasters conference in Vancouver in 2017. I enjoy international gatherings as the cultural differences of the people you meet offer new insights. I was invited to a European table for dinner and really enjoyed the evening in the company of Swiss, French, Italian, and other guests.

The experience of being a Toastmaster significantly increased my public speaking abilities and it was also an enjoyable pastime. I felt it important to take this theory and do something with it in the real world. The opportunity came when TEDx Abbotsford invited me to be a speaker at their event at the University of the Fraser Valley in 2019 where the theme was "Reimagine." The steps leading up to this event were the following: I put giving a TEDx talk as part of my 100 Life Visions in 2013, and in 2018 I placed it on my annual goal for 2019.

The objective was to educate the audience on principles I have learned in my career for managing investments along with innovative ways of adding value to these portfolios.

I researched early in 2019 which locations would be the most feasible to give this talk. There were two: one in Abbotsford, BC and one in Seattle, WA. I only applied to Abbotsford since logistics were better. I was interviewed in the spring and received acceptance while I was in Cambodia in July. Upon returning from Asia I set my goal to give an outstanding talk thinking that I may leverage off it for potential further speaking engagements. I spent three months fine-tuning and memorizing my TEDx talk. My coach, Johann who lives between Canada and Switzerland, was played a part my success as he provided good ideas on the structure of the presentation.

My speech "Passion, beauty, creativity and how to beat the market" was very well received, and I knew the three months of preparation for a fifteen-minute speech had paid off. After getting off stage, someone asked me for my autograph, which was a unique request, so I happily offered it. If you wish to do a second TEDx talk you must come up with fresh content, so you cannot go around the world giving the same speech.

I loved standing on the big red dot,
TEDx Abbotsford, 2019

If you are interested in doing a TEDx talk, you should most importantly have an idea to share and then develop your public speaking ability to a competent level though an organization like Toastmasters.

Making a Difference

My high school had the motto, "a man for others" - to look for ways to make a difference to your family, community, and the world. You have your own capacity to contribute either through service or money. Being open to what is around you allows for endless ways to help others through taking advantage of your strengths. Deciding up to three areas to contribute is a good way to focus. If Elon Musk can run Tesla, SpaceX, and Solar City, among other ventures, then there is room in your life to concurrently get involved in worthy initiatives.

CHAPTER NINE

MONEY - A MEANS TO YOUR VISIONS

"It is better to have a permanent income than to be fascinating."

Oscar Wilde

I knew early on that making a good living was important for me to live a life of options. I had numerous interests and I chose something that was not only a passion but also allowed for supporting an expansive lifestyle. I enjoyed architecture, art, and photography, and pursued them all. However, business seemed to offer the best opportunity for creative problem solving, financial success, and freedom. You are shaped by your environment, and growing up I witnessed one of my brothers, who is a fabulous artist, create beautiful pieces yet he had no interest in combining business skills with his talent for art. Similarly, my mother was a superb artist but did not have a great interest in business, so the income from her work was nominal. Also, my sister wove very nice handbags and she once rented a booth at a crafts convention in Montreal where she reported modest results. I therefore perceived that pursuing art, as a career seemed risky at best. In retrospect I now know that artistic ability combined with solid managerial skills and vision can lead to great things in the art world. It is still difficult but an excellent living can be made with a correct balance of these three essential skills or a combination of people who have these abilities. I met an official portrait artist for the Canadian Government, and looked at her brochure I found it was very professional and with okay art. I thought my artist brother could paint better, but getting these commissions went beyond the artistic talent and required business skills, possibly political ones as well. So being a good artist with the other pieces of the puzzle intact can beat a brilliant artist who lacks the other critical ingredients.

It was during university that I first started to invest. My first investment was a 100-ounce bar of silver purchased from summer job savings when I was 20. I could not keep it long however, as I needed to sell it to pay for university tuition. I caught an upswing in the price of the metal and sold it at a profit. After this introduction, I started investing in the stock market, and before cell phones started becoming common, I would get calls at my university from my stockbroker, which seemed to impress the administration staff. With my brokerage account I invested into options with the potential to have leveraged returns on small capital investments. The problem with buying naked options is that you have to be right in the direction of the underlying security and within the timeframe before expiry. The latter makes it very difficult to make money doing this. In contrast, writing options is a way to lower risk on your stock positions by generating income, which is normally a more prudent approach. It was in 1982 when this all started. Early on I was considering going into the investment industry; however, after the experience of seeing invested money both made and lost, I needed to take a break from that world until I knew it better. I entered the computer world until I would revisit investments a dozen years later with far better designed systems to manage risk.

Financial Independence

In 1997, the year I started in the investment industry, I wrote a cheque to myself thinking at the time that the amount was the minimum net worth I would be comfortable with as a goal, and I tacked the cheque above my desk. Factoring in inflation, that amount was realized by 2016. In retrospect I had set my ambition too low. With a systematic investment plan and living in the Vancouver area with its high real estate prices on a global scale, it is very feasible to achieve some wealth. This, combined with my profession where I developed and invested into my Six Investment ModelsTM further facilitated the growth of our portfolios. What is the right amount of wealth? In my mind, anyone who owns a home, whether it is a studio apartment or mansion, and has no debt but adequate income to support their lifestyle is well off. My material requirements were essentially to have a home, a cottage on a lake, and a vehicle. Having liquidity to support your lifestyle should be an objective once the life necessities are met. You can argue to set your financial ambitions at much higher levels, and this is fine as long as wealth is a way to support your life's visions and to make a difference on a grander scale. Elon Musk and Bill Gates are two role models for innovation with their skills and wealth.

Emotions and Investing

Investing may be an emotional roller coaster where feelings may go from optimism to euphoria, to fear and then panic! Human nature overwhelms most investors. Instead, look at an Apollonian, ordered, time-tested, rules-based system to conquer your emotions when investing and leave any Dionysian intuitive spontaneity for other aspects of your life.

You need to conquer yourself in order to conquer the markets.

Investing Revisited

If you define performance of an investment over a length of time as the metrics for success, there are commonalities among the highest performers in the industry. They include: Jim Simons, George Soros, Peter Lynch, Warren Buffet, and Ray Dalio. They all have Ivy League or other higher education. Is their success due to this advanced education, the contact game among the establishment, or being very bright to make it into these universities? Likely it is a combination of all three. Interestingly the investment methodology is vastly different among these managers, e.g. Jim Simons, quantitative and momentum derived with very short-term daily trades, while on the other end of the spectrum is Warren Buffet with a long-term value approach philosophy which details the use of punching a hole every time you buy an investment and allowing for just 20 holes for your entire life.

Asset Allocation

The investment world has changed in the last two decades. Here are what market indexes returned in different ends of the decade timeframes to achieve the same 7.0% rate of return:

1999 – 100% bonds with 5.0% volatility

2009 – 43% bonds, 27% equity, and 30% alternatives with 12.2% volatility

2019 – 28% bonds, 38% equity, and 34% alternatives with 14% volatility[2]

Bonds comprise both domestic and global fixed income. Equities include: North American, international and emerging markets. Alternatives include: tactical asset allocation, private equity, global real estate, global infrastructure, and precious metals.

A good way to begin designing a portfolio is to imagine dividing a pie into three pieces: fixed income, equities, and alternatives. You will be one step towards a pension fund level of sophistication.

The asset allocation may be included in an Investment Policy Statement (IPS) to record objectives and any restrictions on how an investment portfolio will be managed.

Six Investment Models™

In my career of managing investments, I decided early on that I would focus on Six Investment Models™ The evolution in the models was a constant exercise in researching and refining and adapting appropriate strategies to offer value. After more than two decades of being in the industry, the models were optimized to be the following:

Fixed Income

Model 1: All Income

How should fixed income be invested? I will outline two approaches that work to achieve the lower risk objective of all income.

a. Laddered Guaranteed Investment Certificates (GICs). Laddering one, two, three, four, and five years allows for one GIC to mature every year offering liquidity, and the opportunity to renew for another five years.

b. A combination of government bonds and higher yielding corporate bonds.

When yields are low, why is there even a fixed income component? This is due to the benefit of portfolio stability. Bonds normally perform differently than stocks, and in a bear market, may offer both stability and the ability to move some of the fixed income funds into the equity market when conditions warrant, allowing for rebalancing. With low yields, fixed income may be minimized within an acceptable range of an IPS.

Equities

The Equities piece of the asset allocation pie may be divided into four main categories: Seasonal Rotation, Pension Fund Approach, Growing Dividends, and Momentum.

Model 2: Seasonal Rotation

A century of data shows that almost all of the stock market returns occur over the November to April timeframe while almost no returns from May to October; this is not true every year but most years. This phenomenon occurs in markets around the world, and many academic studies have tried to pinpoint a reason for this market behaviour. The fascinating difference of investing over the summer compared to the winter is also known as "sell in May and go away." By being invested fully in growth companies in the winter while being in cash in the summer, you may improve a portfolio's risk reward profile.

If in 1950 $10,000 was invested only in the summer seasonality (May to October) until the end of October 2019, the portfolio only grew to $20,839; if instead the funds were deployed only in the winter (November to April) until the end of April 2020 then the portfolio grew to $755,595.[3] You can see here that the risk reward of investing in the summer months is not normally favourable. "When researchers focused on 10-year periods they found this strategy beat the market 92% of time."[4]

Why does this phenomenon exit? It may have originated at a time when investors would take the summer off to go to the country and play tennis or golf and return in the fall to the city and begin investing again. Regardless of the nebulous reason, what is important is that it exists. This is one of the most interesting ways to invest on a risk-adjusted basis, since most of the stock market crashes occur in the summer period, so if you can get virtually the entire market return by being invested in only half of the year then you are taking half of the risk to obtain an entire year's worth of returns.

Model 3: Pension Fund Approach

This structure is influenced by how pension funds manage their portfolios with the same sophisticated protocols that may be applied to individual investors. You do not need a billion dollars to have money that is managed as if you did. The long history of the markets illustrates that not one asset class or style of investing always outperforms. By diversifying across a mix of various investment approaches, including asset classes, styles, and managers you can lower portfolio risk. Further, by utilizing tactical asset allocation allows for the movement of funds between the different classes depending on market conditions.

The first step in taking this all-encompassing approach is to divide a pie into three pieces: Fixed Income, Equities, and Alternatives. Next, each piece has subsets, e.g. fixed income includes both government and corporate bonds; equities include both growth and value investment styles along with geographical diversification; and alternatives may include: tactical global asset allocation, infrastructure, real estate, private equity, and precious metals.

Due to this approach often having a higher percentage of equity relative to fixed income and alternatives, this model is classified here under the category of equities. It is understood that fixed income and/or alternatives may have a larger percentage of a portfolio.

Model 4: Growing Dividends

We know from a long track record of investing in equity markets that over half of the total return may be attributed to the dividends. It is therefore prudent to focus on companies that pay a dividend. When you compare investing over three decades, you can see how different approaches yield different results. If you were only to invest into companies that <u>do not</u> pay a dividend, the stunning result is that there would be a -0.2% negative return after 30 years of investing ending December 31, 2019! If you reasonably reject this approach, you can look at the overall TSX market over the same period that returned a respectable 7.9%. Now what if you instead choose only dividend paying companies? Then the returns would be substantially higher at 9.8%. Taking this one step further and narrowing down companies that grow their dividends would result in a much higher 11.1%. Looking deeper by selecting certain dividend growers like Fortis, an electrical generation company, where returns were recorded even higher again at 12.8%![5] Here, you can see that companies that pay a dividend do so because they have strong balance sheets. Dividends also return part of your original investment, which lowers the risk of the purchase in the first place.

Here are some guidelines when putting together a dividend portfolio. Choose only companies that grow their dividends, and see how these companies performed in previous market crashes. Have a preference to the names that either had lower downsides than the market or even had positive returns during market stress.

Utilities are usually considered lower risk in the equity spectrum, historically offering a rewarding combination of lower risk with higher return.

Model 5: Momentum Rotation

Investing with momentum is a methodology of purchasing securities with the highest relative performance over the previous three to twelve months and rotating the weakest performers out of the portfolio. This is done because some stocks trend and continue to do so at least for a while. Wave action in the ocean is an appropriate analogy. You ride a wave as it builds and continues to rise, and then as it peaks and rolls over, you ride the next wave and the process is repeated.

There are variations of momentum strategies. In a 2019 momentum article indexes comprising CDN Bonds, CDN, US and International stocks were ranked every month based on the past twelve months of performance. All funds were then rotated into the one best performing index each month. This approach had a 63.9% relative outperformance to buying and holding the same indexes.[6] I use another momentum stock-based strategy that I had learned from "Investing on Autopilot" where in turn it was learned from research by Steve Foerster, a professor at the University of Western Ontario.

Using the system outlined in Foerster's methodology, choosing a database of 100 of the largest capitalised Canadian or US Small capitalized companies is a starting point that may be derived from the S&P/TSX Composite in Canada or a small cap index in the US. From this initial list of 100, only the top 10 equal-weighted securities passes based on price performance over the last 12 months, known as the formation period. Then every three months, known as the holding period, the list is resorted again based on 12 months' performance, and the new top 10 stocks are selected. In the original study the previous quarter performance is given a double weighting, i.e. the first three quarters are given 20% weighting each and the final quarter is given a 40% weighting to capture the more recent price gains. Typically, one half of the stocks are changed in the three months' rotation, although there may be more or less than this. In a momentum study by Foerster, Prihar, and Schmitz, a five-year research study from 1977-1992, illustrated an annual performance of 33.2% before transaction costs.[7] This performance was found while the TSE total return index at that time returned 13.1%. Outperformance was shown to exist in Canada, the US, and Europe, with Canada having the highest returns. The elegance of this way of investing is that the stock price's relative strength tells us where we should invest as the market factors in the demand characteristics that fundamental analysis may not fully pick up on. On a follow-up study by Foerster in 1998, performance net of fees from 1993 – 2nd quarter of 1998 illustrated a 27.0% return compared to the TSE300 14.5%.[8]

In running a momentum strategy, you need to be patient, have the discipline to not second guess the data, maintain the strategy in weak periods, and have a long-term investment time horizon of ideally five years or longer.

Interestingly the highest recorded and audited performance of an investment manager is Jim Simons of Renaissance Technologies in the US with an annualized return of 39.1% from 1988 – 2018.

His Medallion fund performance is net of an average of 27.0% annual fees (yes, 27.0%); therefore, the gross returns before fees was 66.1% over the three decades.[9] His company also uses momentum, using very short-term computerized trading systems.

Alternatives

Model 6: Alternatives

In low interest rate environments alternative investing has taken the place of a portion of fixed income in portfolios in an effort to find higher returns without being exposed to excessive risk. Alternatives invest into securities that offer non-correlated returns to fixed income and equities. Real estate, commodities, and tactical asset allocation would be examples. Here we can lower risk by having investments that may earn more than fixed income while diversifying a portfolio beyond traditional asset classes. If you were to choose only one alternative strategy a global tactical asset allocation approach would be a solid candidate. Here, you have the capacity investments to move between fixed income, equities, and other asset classes, like commodities or currencies depending on market conditions.

Precious metals are another solid choice in the alternative category. Like buying fire insurance, gold bullion may offer a hedge in certain market events, especially inflationary and even deflationary ones in nature. A good combination is one of precious metals streaming companies, ones that process gold rather than not mine them, and gold bullion whether trading on a stock exchange or physically held.

A 10% asset allocation in precious metals may be sufficient to give additional portfolio diversification and risk mitigation.

Sustainable Investing

Investors increasingly want to have their values represented in their portfolios. Sustainable investing or Environmental, Social, Governance (ESG) screening has shown to add some performance in most studies according to a report by Carleton University in 2015. Screening may be positive or negative. An example of a negative screen may be against a company that is not up to date in its pollution control systems. An example of a positive screen may be a company in favour of renewable energy with a focus on solar, wind, and hydro. There are compelling companies that demonstrate both sustainability and well above market rates of returns.

How Younger Investors May Build a $1 Million Portfolio

How can a young investor make a difference to his or her family, community and the world when the cost of living is a challenge, especially in expensive housing markets? There are ways to adapt and thrive. By contributing $500 a month to a tax-free savings account (TFSA in Canada) there are various possible outcomes assuming a starting age of 23. An aggressive approach that generates 15% should achieve a one-million-dollar portfolio by the time the investor is 45. A moderate but all equity approach focused on growing dividends that achieves 10% may see the million by 52. And what if the investor took a conservative model that returns only 5%? Even then a one-million-dollar nest egg may be achieved by a retirement age of 67.

Portfolio	Age	Return	Value
Aggressive	45	15%	$1,099,007
Moderate	52	10%	$1,085,661
Conservative	67	5%	$1,006,111

See Appendix D for detailed Tax-Free Savings Account (TFSA) scenarios.

Real Estate

Home

I bought my first house in 1988 when I was 26 in Pointe-Claire South, a suburb of Montreal. It was an early life goal to own my own place. Interest rates were high at the time and I had a good career but limited equity. A friend Stan, who was a real estate agent I knew from university, helped structure a deal so I was able to buy the home.

My first house at 58 Waverley Road, in Pointe-Claire, 1988, since demolished.

The neighbourhood had a charming country feeling, as originally the area was a cottage area for people who lived in the city. Although the home was modest and needing renovation, the lot was 15,000 sq. ft. with mature trees. The house was replaced in 2020 with a new home taking advantage of the large lot. The tax-free nature of a home, at least in Canada, makes this the most important investment most people make. The lifestyle of owning a place is valuable in a non-monetary way as it allows us freedom in managing our living space.

An element of due diligence that I have found to work in many cases of purchasing real estate is to knock on the doors of immediate neighbours to: 1. Introduce yourself; 2. Get to know who the closest neighbours are; and, 3. Learn things about your potential purchase. What you can find out from the above is often valuable to determine whether or not to proceed with a transaction. Once when we were looking at a condominium purchase, I knocked on the neighbouring door and a lady opened the door with so much cigarette smoke billowing out that it reminded me of some bars I went to in university. Since her balcony was adjacent to the unit I was looking at, it was clear that smoke would be part of the package. We passed on the purchase.

Cottage

A country cottage as a second residence is more of a lifestyle purchase as there are likely better ways to generate wealth, including dividend-producing investments or rental properties. So why would you own one? We all have our passions, and some people collect exotic cars, travel, or garden. Although budgets and finances need to be scrutinized in making a cottage decision, not everything

Outdoor physical activity followed by a swim and time on your dock is paradise, 2020

comes down to what might make you the most amount of money. To swim in front of your dock, have a gathering spot for your family and friends, enjoy some privacy, and have a lifetime of memories is priceless. It is good to be able to go somewhere else no matter how pleasant your principal residence is.

> ***A cottage should ideally be within three hours from your principal residence.***

Investment

Positive cash flow is the name of the game. By buying properties with a minimal down payment, e.g. 20%, and arranging the balance to be financed with the rental income will allow leverage in your investments. A general rule is for the rental income to cover the expenses, and sell in a seller's market when there is a significant rise in value of the original investment. You can expand a portfolio of rental apartments this way. This is most feasible where the price of real estate is lower while there is still rental demand. This combination may likely mean finding these opportunities in towns away from where you live. If you are fortunate to live in a place where these characteristics are already apparent, then that is a significant advantage in being able to manage the properties. A property manager can be a useful part of the team to handle many of the tasks needed to manage both the properties and tenants.

In growing a real estate portfolio, narrow down to no more than three areas to invest in and then have three property managers who can handle the entire portfolio.

CHAPTER TEN

SPIRITUALITY – YOUR INNER JOURNEY

"Those who look outside dream, those who look inside awake."

Carl Jung

There is a broad spectrum when looking through the lens of a spiritual life. It may or may not be religious, and in both cases you may be awestruck by the grand sophistication of the universe. In appreciating the infinite, Buddhists state that "if you do not desire you do not suffer." A related healthy attitude is to be at peace with yourself. This philosophy does not mean to abandon your human aspirations but put them into context of a far greater realm. Have the imagination and open-mindedness to the vast mystery of the universe.

Do not live a scarcity mindset but instead have a philosophy of abundance.

Being in the moment

Eckart Tolle's "The Power of Now, a Guide to Spiritual Enlightenment" was one of the most powerful spiritual books I ever read. The clarity in how it describes how you are not the thinker but something much greater than that had such impact on me that I had to put the book down and absorb the profound insights when I first read it. The book emphasizes the importance of being present and not allowing the mind identified self from taking over our being. To see the mind as one of many instruments in a toolbox allows you to put into perspective that you are much more than your mind. By watching down over yourself, you can see beyond the physical realm and understand that you are much more than your physicality. In more established historical and timeless spiritual works, there also are profound messages where you have to prepare to dig though parables to discover the hidden meanings.

Positive Attitude

Since you are alive you survived the chess game of biology, and by nature's standards you are a winner of the evolutionary battle. A good periodic reminder is to be thankful and not take for granted the life you have while you continue your daily efforts to better yourself and by extension, humanity. Success and failures are both just experiences to learn from, and failures may teach you more valuable lessons than living a life without struggles. Forgiveness to others and to yourself brings healing. An exercise of self-examination may be useful to determine strengths and weaknesses, but also, take a look at yourself from the outside and allow an appreciation of who you are at your best. You may find areas within yourself for improvement. By observing your traits, without judgment, you can be prepared to stand on a solid footing, allowing for growth and building on whatever foundation you have.

One of my martial arts instructors was also a professor of philosophy at the University of Toronto, once said that everything comes down to attitude. Since he did not think everyone would believe this, he said, "95% is due to attitude." Without quibbling on the percentage, it is healthier to have a positive can-do mindset than a defeatist victim identity of yourself.

Meditation

In high school my class visited a monastery in the countryside and we had the chance to be alone in a small room and meditate. I tried this but was not ready for it as I had a lot of nervous energy, and I could not find a way to benefit from this exercise at the time. Much later in

Reflective moment and enjoying the Mission Hill Winery, Kelowna, 2017

life I better recognized the value in taking time to calm the mind and run though meditation exercises. Today with meditation apps, it's much easier to follow different programs that best suit your temperament and the depth of experience that you seek.

Openness to your true self

Whenever you are in a situation that is unhealthy, such as in a job that is not a good match, or a personal relationship that is out of sync with who you are, then you have three choices in dealing with a conflict: fix it, remove yourself from it, or live with it. Option three is not for an enlightened person to perpetually live in conflict. This leaves the other two options of finding a solution or leaving the situation for a better opportunity. Once a decision is made pursue it with resolve.

Tackle life with reflection and action on terms that you deem to be true to yourself.

Interconnectedness

Scientists write that 50,000 years ago a mass cataclysm affected the earth likely through a meteor strike or vast volcanic eruptions, which reduced the total Homo sapiens population to less than five thousand. We are all descended from this small group, and if a generation is 25 years long then we all have only 2,000 direct ancestors to these small tribes in Africa. We are not only closely connected but we are only 2% genetically different from chimpanzees. Recognizing our shared humanity each with our own struggles is a lot healthier than looking at superficial, racial or political differences. Seeing our common heritage opens the gateway to enhance the human, social, and ecological connections, without which humanity is at risk.

Learning

Review the works of great spiritual masters, whether they are from antiquity or contemporary. Timeless and well thought out wisdom comes from historical texts, which are worthy of refection. There are thousands of years of wisdom that offer grounding in context of your brief life.

"It is not the critic who counts, not the person who points out how the strong stumbled or where the doer of deeds could have done better. The credit belongs to the person who is actually in the arena whose face is marked by dust and sweat and blood who strives valiantly, who knows the great enthusiasm, the great devotion, and spends himself in a worthy cause who at the best knows in the end the triumph of high achievement and who at the worst, if he fails, at least fails while doing greatly so that his place shall never be with those cold and timid souls who know neither victory nor defeat."

Teddy Roosevelt

EPILOGUE

In pursuing your visions, dreams, and life, you will have your own unique HEROISMS. If there are any insights that motivate you to action, then I trust your time was well spent to help explore your own roadmap. Although I came up with the idea for HEROISMS more than six years before bringing this book to fruition, it is perhaps appropriate since so much has happened in the past years that allowed for more material, e.g. raising our two daughters, the building of our lakefront cottage, TEDx speech, the growth of my wealth management practice, writing, singing and recording "Cottage Life," and building a "Temple of Love."

The dock was the first project as most of the cottage life experience is outdoors. This photo made it to the front cover of Cottage magazine, July/August 2012.

As I write I am not yet finished with my own pursuit of living a full life, and I still have to tackle more of my 100 Life Visions. As I am in good health if I focus on two a year it is possible that I may hit 100, and if so great, and if not, the reward is in the journey, robust in passion, beauty, and creativity. At a certain point in your voyage, you will transition to savouring the life you have built, and any new initiatives may function in areas that work best for where you are in the seasonality of life.

ABOUT THE AUTHOR

Peter Boronkay grew up in Montreal and Boston, spent summers in Vermont, and studied at Loyola, a private preparatory school before he graduated with a B. Comm. from Concordia University. Peter is engaged as an Associate Portfolio Manager and Partner at an office of Raymond James Ltd. in Vancouver, BC. He holds a Chartered Financial Planner (CFP), and Canadian Investment Manager (CIM) designations. Peter developed a unique system of Six Investment Models™ that helps clients as well as advisors remove emotion and focus on rational judgment in the investment decision-making process. Peter is a TEDx speaker and his volunteer focus in sport is reflected by his long-standing involvement with the investment committee at Golf Canada, his past role of Director of Finance at the Canadian Paralympic Committee, and as a graduate of the Olympic Academy of Canada. Peter's own athletic highlight was both as founder and player on a Canadian curling team that won gold at an international curling tournament in Europe. Outside of his profession, Peter and his family enjoy cottage life at a lake on the Sunshine Coast, BC.

APPENDIX

A: 100 Life Visions

1	2Education	Loyola High School diploma	5/1/1979
2	5Interests	Bronze Medallion	12/8/1979
3	2Education	Vanier College Dip. Sciences	1/1/1982
4	5Interests	Hungary, Austria trip	8/1/1983
5	5Interests	Run 42 km marathon	9/1/1983
6	2Education	B. Comm., Concordia U.	5/1/1985
7	5Interests	Ski in Austria	2/1/1986
8	5Interests	White-water rafting guide	5/1/1987
9	5Interests	Martial Arts training in Japan	11/1/1987
10	5Interests	Martial Arts - Brown belt	12/1/1987
11	6Society	Calgary Olympics volunteer	2/1/1988
12	7Money	1st house, Pointe-Claire, QC	10/31/1988
13	5Interests	Martial Arts U of Conn. 1st	11/1/1988
14	2Education	Architecture U of Colorado	9/1/1989
15	3Relations	Unity of souls, marry Geraldine	7/21/1990
16	5Interests	Luge - slide, Calgary track	2/1/1993
17	5Interests	National Lifeguard Service	12/1/1993
18	5Interests	Mexico - Mayan ruins	2/1/1994
19	5Interests	Greater Vancouver Book contr.	1/1/1995
20	2Education	Canadian Securities Course	8/1/1996
21	3Relations	First child – Francesca	11/29/1996
22	4Occupation	Career in Investments	5/1/1997

23	4Occupation	Article in Globe and Mail	8/21/1997
24	4Occupation	Column in newspaper	1/1/1998
25	5Interests	Hawaii – Scuba dive	3/21/1998
26	3Relations	Second child – Selena	2/19/1999
27	7Money	2nd house, Bowen Island, BC	8/1/1999
28	5Interests	Hungary travels	8/1/2001
29	5Interests	Italy - Cinque Terra hike	8/1/2001
30	5Interests	Swam 7km+ Sakinaw Lake, BC	8/29/2001
31	2Education	CDN Investment Manager	10/1/2001
32	3Relations	Up to 5 close friendships 25 yr	1/1/2002
33	4Occupation	Manage $20M+ (Phase I)	1/1/2002
34	2Education	Fellow CDN Securities Institute	5/1/2002
35	2Education	Certified Financial Planner	9/11/2002
36	3Relations	Published father's books – 2	1/1/2004
37	6Society	Olympic Academy of Canada	7/1/2004
38	5Interests	Chatterbox Falls, BC	8/1/2004
39	7Money	3rd house with ocean views	10/1/2005
40	5Interests	My curling team wins gold	12/1/2005
41	6Society	Torino Paralympics guest	2/1/2006
42	3Relations	Manoir Westmount-mother	5/1/2007
43	6Society	Director of Finance, CPC	10/1/2007
44	6Society	Met President Bill Clinton	11/1/2007
45	3Relations	Art show for my mother	11/9/2007
46	5Interests	Shoot at a firing range	12/1/2007
47	7Money	Build gazebo with ocean views	7/1/2008
48	5Interests	Walk on Great Wall of China	9/1/2008
49	6Society	Beijing Paralympics - guest	9/1/2008
50	6Society	COC B member/Supporter	1/5/2009
51	5Interests	Sing in a choir	1/12/2009

52	5Interests	Sail to Jedediah Island, BC	7/25/2009
53	5Interests	Ski torch parade New Year's	12/31/2009
54	6Society	2010 Olympic Cer. Perform	2/28/2010
55	3Relations	2010 Daughters contribution	3/12/2010
56	5Interests	Horseback riding, Flying U	8/10/2010
57	5Interests	Lakefront acreage with dock	8/12/2010
58	5Interests	Play Greensleeves on piano	10/1/2011
59	5Interests	Run equiv 6,521k (Canada)	12/31/2012
60	4Occupation	Partner of Investment firm	6/1/2013
61	5Interests	Italy – Rome	7/13/2013
62	5Interests	Pick up Stanley Cup trophy	9/6/2013
63	4Occupation	Invented HEROISMS concept	1/1/2014
64	7Money	Build timber frame cottage	8/14/2014
65	6Society	Ann. cottage event for friends	9/1/2014
66	6Society	President - Toastmasters club	6/1/2015
67	3Relations	Geraldine and I – (25 yrs.+)	7/21/2015
68	4Occupation	Learn words 25 languages	7/1/2016
69	5Interests	Canoe the Forest Lake Loop	7/6/2016
70	7Money	Financial independence	8/1/2016
71	5Interests	Barbados	11/6/2016
72	5Interests	Compose "Cottage Life" song	12/27/2016
73	6Society	Distinguished Toastmaster	6/14/2017
74	5Interests	Learn to ride a motorcycle	1/3/2018
75	5Interests	Create an orchard	5/1/2018
76	4Occupation	Manage $50M (Phase II)	12/24/2018
77	5Interests	Thailand, Cambodia	7/1/2019
78	3Relations	Siblings – Swiss settlement	9/1/2019
79	6Society	TEDx talk	11/9/2019
80	4Occupation	Portfolio Management reg.	12/1/2019

81	5Interests	South Pacific trip - gift	12/25/2019
82	4Occupation	Write HEROISMS	12/31/2019
83	3Relations	Finance daughters univ. educ.	12/31/2019
84	1Health	5kms runs into my 70's+	
85	2Education	Course - Harvard/Oxford	
86	2Education	Learn Spanish	
87	4Occupation	Manage $100M (Phase III)	
88	5Interests	Buenos Aries, learn tango	
89	5Interests	Dubai - Burj Al Arab	
90	5Interests	Egypt – Temples	
91	5Interests	Europe castle bike tour	
92	5Interests	Live internationally 1+ yrs	
93	5Interests	Olympia, run ancient track	
94	5Interests	Capri, Swim Blue Grotto	
95	5Interests	Opera in a historical setting	
96	5Interests	Read 11 vol Story of Civilization	
97	5Interests	Turkey - Istanbul	
98	5Interests	Dine at House of Lords. London	
99	5Interests	Run Olympic torch relay	
100	4Occupation	Teach next generation of wealth advisor	

B: Health History

PERSONAL PARAMETERS

Name:

Blood Type:

Height & Weight:

BMI (Body Mass Index) = Weight (kgs)/Height (metres)^2

Waist circumference:

Blood Pressure:

Resting Heart rate:

MEDICAL HISTORY

Personal Medical History:

Medications:

Allergies:

Surgical History:

Family History:

MEDICAL SCREENING & PREVENTION

Hematology Profile:

Lipid Profile (Cholesterol):

Metabolic Profile (f-glucose/HbA1C/TSH):

Colon Rectal Screening:

Eye Test:

Prostrate Screening (Men)/Breast & Pelvic Screening (Women):

Skin Screen:

Mental Health Wellness and Cognitive Screening:

Urine Testing:

Immunization and other Travel Vaccines for Adults:

Shingles, Tetanus, Pertussis, Pneumonia

C: Countries Visited

Bold font for places lived in longer than 4 months.

Number	Country	Province/State
1	Austria	
2	Barbados	
3	Cambodia	
4	**Canada**	
		Alberta
		British Columbia
		Manitoba
		New Brunswick
		Nova Scotia
		Ontario
		Québec
		Saskatchewan
5	Costa Rica	
6	Cuba	
7	China	
8	France	
9	Germany	
10	Vatican City	
11	Hungary	
12	Italy	
13	Japan	
14	Malta	
15	Mexico	

16	Monaco	
17	Netherlands	
18	Poland	
19	Switzerland	
20	Taiwan	
21	Thailand	
22	United Kingdom	
23	**United States**	
		Arizona
		California
		Colorado
		Connecticut
		Florida
		Georgia
		Hawaii
		Idaho
		Illinois
		Indiana
		Iowa
		Kansas
		Louisiana
		Maine
		Massachusetts
		Michigan
		Minnesota
		Montana
		New Hampshire
		New Mexico

		Ohio
		Oklahoma
		Oregon
		Texas
		Utah
		Vermont
		Washington
		Wisconsin
		Wyoming

Countries, places, experiences for future consideration

	Argentina	Buenos Aries, learn the tango
	Austria	Lake Hallestattersee, Vienna Opera Ball
	Croatia	Rovini, Hotel Mulini
	Dubai	Burj Al Arab -good on New Year's
	Egypt	Abu Simbel, Eskaleh, Nubian Ecolodge
	Europe	Christmas Markets
	Europe	Tour of castles (bicycle)
	Europe	Venice Simpleton Orient Express
	Fiji	Archepelo resort
	France	Chateau Margoux vineyard
	Greece	Olympia, run ancient Olympic track
	Greece	Meteora monastery and Lessaly
	Israel	Jerusalem
	Italy	Capri, swim into the Blue grotto
	Italy	Lake Como, Villa d'Este
	Italy	Montastero Santa Rose Conca dei Marini

	Jordan	Petra
	Nepal	Hike the Himalayas, Chilcot Trail
	Netherlands	Amertand, houseboat on canals
	Peru	Hike the Inca Trail to Machu Pichu
	Spain	Alhambra, Granada, Alcazar-Segovia
	Switzerland	Train ride of the Glacier Express
	Turkey	Agor-Cappalocie, Hippodrome, Uchuar
	UK	Scotland, St. Andrew's golf
	UK	London, Dine at House of Lords
	UK	Wimbledon (July)

D: Tax-free Savings Account Scenarios

Age	Year	%	$	%	$	%	$	Ann.
23	2020	5	6,300	10	6,600	15	6,900	6,000
24	2021	5	12,915	10	13,860	15	14,835	6,000
25	2022	5	19,861	10	21,846	15	23,960	6,000
26	2023	5	27,154	10	30,631	15	34,454	6,000
27	2024	5	34,811	10	40,294	15	46,522	6,000
28	2025	5	42,852	10	50,923	15	60,401	6,000
29	2026	5	51,295	10	62,615	15	76,361	6,000
30	2027	5	60,159	10	75,477	15	94,715	6,000
31	2028	5	69,467	10	89,625	15	115,822	6,000
32	2029	5	79,241	10	105,187	15	140,096	6,000
33	2030	5	89,503	10	122,306	15	168,010	6,000
34	2031	5	100,278	10	141,136	15	200,112	6,000
35	2032	5	111,592	10	161,850	15	237,028	6,000
36	2033	5	123,471	10	184,635	15	279,482	6,000
37	2034	5	135,945	10	209,698	15	328,305	6,000
38	2035	5	149,042	10	237,268	15	384,451	6,000
39	2036	5	162,794	10	267,595	15	449,018	6,000
40	2037	5	177,234	10	300,955	15	523,271	6,000
41	2038	5	192,396	10	337,650	15	608,661	6,000
42	2039	5	208,316	10	378,015	15	706,861	6,000
43	2040	5	225,031	10	422,416	15	819,790	6,000
44	2041	5	242,583	10	471,258	15	949,658	6,000
45	2042	5	261,012	10	524,984	15	1,099,007	6,000
46	2043	5	280,363	10	584,082	15	1,270,758	6,000

47	2044	5	300,681	10	649,091	15	1,468,272	6,000
48	2045	5	322,015	10	720,600	15	1,695,413	6,000
49	2046	5	344,415	10	799,260	15	1,956,624	6,000
50	2047	5	367,936	10	885,786	15	2,257,018	6,000
51	2048	5	392,633	10	980,964	15	2,602,471	6,000
52	2049	5	418,565	10	1,085,661	15	2,999,742	6,000
53	2050	5	445,793	10	1,200,827	15	3,456,603	6,000
54	2051	5	474,383	10	1,327,509	15	3,981,993	6,000
55	2052	5	504,402	10	1,466,860	15	4,586,192	6,000
56	2053	5	535,922	10	1,620,146	15	5,281,021	6,000
57	2054	5	569,018	10	1,788,761	15	6,080,074	6,000
58	2055	5	603,769	10	1,974,237	15	6,998,985	6,000
59	2056	5	640,257	10	2,178,261	15	8,055,733	6,000
60	2057	5	678,570	10	2,402,687	15	9,270,993	6,000
61	2058	5	718,799	10	2,649,555	15	10,668,542	6,000
62	2059	5	761,039	10	2,921,111	15	12,275,723	6,000
63	2060	5	805,391	10	3,219,822	15	14,123,982	6,000
64	2061	5	851,960	10	3,548,404	15	16,249,479	6,000
65	2062	5	900,858	10	3,909,845	15	18,693,801	6,000
66	2063	5	952,201	10	4,307,429	15	21,504,771	6,000
67	2064	5	1,006,111	10	4,744,772	15	24,737,386	6,000

E: Peace – Fourth Proposed Olympic Pillar

Since 1945 global conflict has been avoided, but barely. We cannot allow ourselves to get complacent about this relative length of peace, and to complement Sports, Culture and the Environment; I propose that "Peace" be added as the fourth noble pillar. It is sobering to remember that the modern Olympics were cancelled five times due to war. Current global pressures that may also threaten games include terrorism, climate change, politics, and economic instability. As in the ancient Olympics peace was arranged first, and then came the Olympic games, not vice versa. Let us be vigilant of this reality.

HISTORY

We know that the origin of the ancient Olympics promoting peace began in 776 BC when these games organized the "Ekecheiria," or Olympic Truce. During this Truce, athletes and members of the public were allowed to travel in complete safety to participate in or attend the Olympic games from their hometown. This tradition of ceasing all hostilities during the Olympic games was respected for twelve centuries of Olympic games history. In more recent times, in 1999, a record 180 United Nations Member-States co-sponsored a resolution in support of observing an Olympic Truce for the subsequent Olympic games.

SPORTS

Why should we look at sports to help foster peace between nations? Because sport contributes to removing barriers between people and offers a rich opportunity for furthering connections that foster positive relationships. We already know that sport contributes to health, economic, and social opportunities especially for our youth. Sport may also foster good-will and tolerance by allowing people to interact across political, religious, and cultural levels that they may not otherwise experience, leading to better awareness and respect between cultures. We celebrate that:

"The International Olympic Committee (IOC) was founded on the belief that sport, especially in an Olympic context, can bring benefits beyond those simply related to physical activity. Sport is a global language. It does not matter where you come from as everyone, given the chance, can speak "Sport!" Sport fosters understanding between individuals, facilitates dialogue between divergent communities and breeds tolerance between nations."[10]

The last four words of the above statement reinforce the importance of peace as an objective and proposed fourth pillar of the Olympic movement.

IOC and the IOTF (International Olympic Truce Foundation)

The groundwork for adding a fourth pillar of peace is already in place since the IOC established the IOTF, and associated centre. This non-governmental organization within the Olympic movement defines its modus operandi around the following goals: "To promote the Olympic ideals to serve peace, friendship and understanding in the world, and in particular, to promote the ancient Greek tradition of the Olympic Truce; To initiate conflict prevention and resolution through sport, culture and the Olympic ideals, by cooperating with all inter and non-governmental organizations specialized in this field, by developing educational and research programmes, and by launching communications campaigns to promote the Olympic Truce. To meet these objectives, the IOTF established the International Olympic Truce Centre (IOTC)"[11]

Since the IOC has already recognized the opportunities to promote peace through its global network, and because there are few more important goals than maintaining relative global security, I propose the fourth pillar to be formalized as "Peace." For this pillar to be more than just an ideal there must be an action plan to actively promote this initiative to the international community. This plan already established by the IOTC, is comprised of: bringing together heads of state, government, and NGO's to promote the Olympic Truce as a tool to prevent or resolve conflict, and to make every available attempt to honour the Olympic Truce during every Olympic Games as a first step in fostering cooperation in context of the principles of the UN. I suggest taking the principle of the Olympic Truce beyond the two-week Olympic games and having a reporting system in place to monitor any extension of the truce beyond the games. Any progress may be disseminated on the IOC website. The IOC has already established three primary objectives to foster observance of the Olympic Truce that may be summarized as: the bringing together of youth for the celebration of Olympic ideals; the use of sport to foster relationships in areas in conflict; and to bring humanitarian help to war torn places.

UNITED NATIONS (UN)

A key component and supporter of peace through sport is the UN. It has the unique ability to provide efficient connections between the various stakeholders where they have common goals such as peace through sport. The UN General Assembly has regularly adopted resolutions that discuss "Building a peaceful and better world through sport and the Olympic Ideal." This action is designed for the members to reflect on the Olympic Truce to pursue those ideals and aspirations that are in line with the principles of the UN Charter for dealing with conflict by using non-violent methods. For many years the UN has acknowledged the relevance of sport in society, and the UN departments already have a history of using famous athletes to bring awareness of humane causes such as health, equality for women, and human rights.

CONCLUSION

Since we understand that risk of conflict between nations may emanate from many different areas including: terrorism, environment, politics, and economic instability, let us as supporters of the Olympic spirit continue to rise to the occasion to help minimize these threats, and continue to leverage the Olympic Games for peace - from two weeks, to one month, and eventually, all year long.

"Olympic ideals are also UN ideals: tolerance, equality, fair play and, most of all, peace. Together, the Olympics and the UN can be a winning team. But the contest will not be won easily. War, intolerance and deprivation continue to stalk the earth. We must

fight back. Just as athletes strive for world records, so must we strive for world peace."[12]

Kofi A. Annan, UN Secretary General

SOURCES

[1] World Curling Federation, printed from the worldcurling.org website, 2015

[2] Russell Investments, December 2019.

[3] P138-140 "Inevitable Wealth", 1950-2014 S&P500 (2015-20 updates by Peter Boronkay)

[4] Mark Hulbert, from www.MarketWatch.com Oct 29, 2010

[5] BMO Global Asset Management Jan 1, 1990 – Dec 31, 2019

[6] Norman Rother, This 'hot potato' portfolio has gained an average of 15.9% annually over nearly four decades, The Globe and Mail, Sept 18, 2019 re. FTSE Canada Universe Bond Index, the S&P/TSX Composite Index, S&P500 and MCSI EAFE Index, Jan 1, 1981 – Aug 30, 2019 $10,000 Invested

[7] Steve Forester, Anoop Prihar, John Schmitz, Back to the Future, Canadian Investment Review, Winter 1994/95

[8] Steve Forester, Momentum Strategies: Catching a Wave, Canadian Moneysaver, Sept. 1998

[9] Gregory Zuckerman, "The Man Who Solved the Market: How Jim Simons Launched the Quant Revolution", 2019

[10] Olympictruce.org

[11] Olympic.org

[12] UN.org

Manufactured by Amazon.ca
Bolton, ON